HOTSPOTS

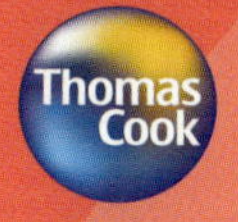

TURKEY
AEGEAN COAST

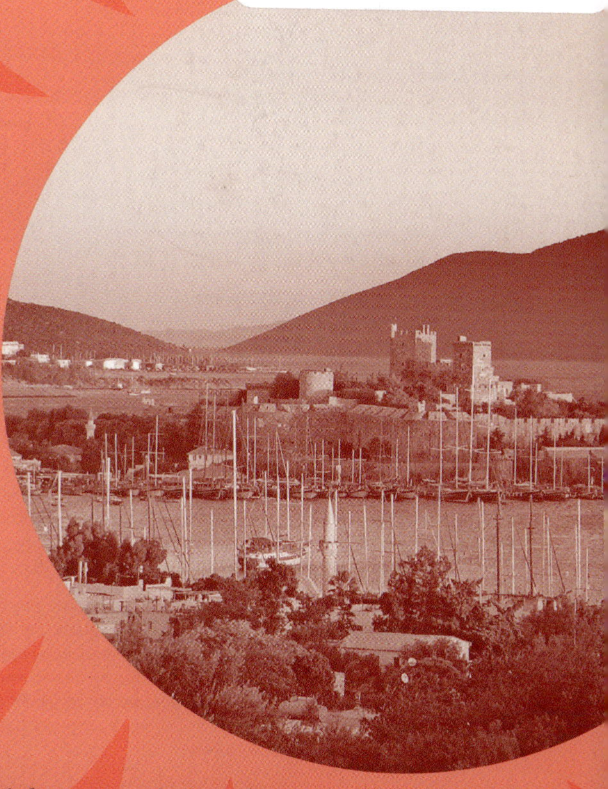

Çeşme, Altinkum, Kuşadasi, Bodrum, Gümbet, The Bodrum Peninsula

Written by Lindsay Bennett
Front cover photography courtesy of Thomas Cook Tour Operations Ltd

Original design concept by Studio 183 Limited
Series design by the Bridgewater Book Company
Cover design/artwork by Lee Biggadike, Studio 183 Limited

Produced by the Bridgewater Book Company
The Old Candlemakers, West Street, Lewes, East Sussex BN7 2NZ, United Kingdom
www.bridgewaterbooks.co.uk
Project Editor: Emily Casey Bailey
Project Designer: Lisa McCormick

Published by Thomas Cook Publishing
A division of Thomas Cook Tour Operations Limited
PO Box 227, Units 15–16, Coningsby Road, Peterborough PE3 8SB, United Kingdom
email: books@thomascook.com
www.thomascookpublishing.com
+ 44 (0) 1733 416477

ISBN-13: 978-1-84157-532-2
ISBN-10: 1-84157-532-1

Head of Thomas Cook Publishing: Chris Young
Project Editor: Diane Ashmore
Production/DTP Editor: Steven Collins

Printed and bound in Spain by Graficas Cems, Navarra, Spain

CONTENTS

SYMBOLS KEY

The following is a key to the symbols used throughout this book:

information office
hospital
restaurant
bus station
police station
café
post office
airport
bar
church
tip
fine dining
train station
shopping

---

telephone
fax
email
website address
address
opening times
important

€ budget price €€ mid-range price €€€ most expensive

★ specialist interest ★★ see if passing ★★★ top attraction

INTRODUCTION

Getting to know Turkey's Aegean coast

Aklepiyon
BERGAMA
SOMA
DIKILI
AKHIS
N
0
250
500 m
0
0.25 mile
FOÇA
MANISA
Dalyan
UŞAK
SMYRNA
TURGUTLU
SALIHLI
IZMIR
Sardis
ÇEŞME
ALAÇATI
ALAŞEHIR
EŞME
Altinkum
Teos
ÖDEMIŞ
Koraka Burnu
TIRE
Vathi
Ephesus
SELÇUK
Kuşadi Korfezi
KUŞADASI
NAZILLI
SARAYKÖY
Hierapolis
Pamukkale
AYDIN
Menderes Valley
SAMOS (GREECE)
BATHY
Priene
SÖKE
Dilek Peninsular
DENIZLI
MILETUS
Bafa Gölü
Heracleia

AEGEAN COAST
Gulf of Gökova
Mandalya Körfezi
LÉROS (GREECE)
KÁLYMNOS (GREECE)
KÖS (GREECE)
Bodrum Peninsula
GÜMBET
BODRUM
MILAS
MUĞLA
Marcal Daglari
Gokovalskefe
Kerme Körfezi
Resadiye Yarimadasi
DATÇA
MARMARIS
Köycegiz Lake
Kaunos
Dalaman Nehri
RHODOS
RHODES (GREECE)
LINDOS
BLACK SEA
TURKEY
AEGEAN COAST
AEGEAN SEA
MEDITERRANEAN SEA
SYRIA

Getting to know Turkey's Aegean coast

What is your idea of the perfect holiday destination? Long, hot sunny days, with beautiful sandy beaches? Crystal clear seas and friendly people? Lots to see and do, but no rush to do anything? Then Turkey's Aegean coast – a touch of spice but with a few touches of home – is the place for you, whether you enjoy 'buzzing' nightlife or a quiet evening with just the buzzing of the cicadas.

A LAND RICH IN HISTORY

'Where East and West meet' or 'The Crossroads of History' – are just two ways to describe this land. Turkey stretches from the Aegean Sea in the west into the Middle East and Asia in the east, and it has been used as a land bridge for hundreds of generations. Persians, Greeks, Romans, Byzantines and Ottomans all feature strongly in its long history and have left fascinating legacies for today's holidaymakers to explore.

VARIED NATURAL BEAUTY

Not a history buff? No worries! Turkey has much more to offer. The sheer beauty of the landscapes would be enough to draw the crowds but here you can do more than simply gaze in awe. A whole fleet of boats cruises just offshore, jeep safaris navigate through forests, river beds and mountain passes, hiking trails point the way to panoramic vistas and you can pilot a jet ski or kayak to explore the coastal shallows.

If this all sounds too energetic, there is plenty of opportunity to bronze on the beach and dip your toes in the azure shallows with a beach bar just on the doorstep for that cooling drink – or you can head to a Turkish bath for a little pampering.

EVENING ENTERTAINMENT

Nightlife is varied here: the coast's larger towns offer some of the most raucous nightlife of any holiday destination in Europe – great foam parties and fishbowl cocktails – while smaller resorts are the perfect locations for romantic meals and moonlit strolls on the beach.

FASCINATING COASTLINE

The Aegean is Turkey's most westerly strip of land and the country's most beautiful and varied coastline. A couple of long peninsulas push out towards Greece, and many islands and islets sit just offshore. Tiny coves contrast with long swathes of sand that have helped this region to become Turkey's most developed tourist area. Kuşadası and the smaller resorts of Altınkum and Gümbet offer sheer energetic holiday fun, while Bodrum still has something of an enigmatic sophistication and Çeşme is a windsurfing Mecca.

The brush strokes of history can be seen on every corner and this region has perhaps the greatest concentration of major ancient sites in Turkey. One of the most famous of these is Ephesus, unique in the Eastern Mediterranean, and the most visited attraction in the country.

AN ANCIENT WAY OF LIFE

Traditional lifestyles have all but disappeared on the coastal strip, but if you head just a little way inland you will discover it is a different matter. You will soon find yourself among farmers and their families. Here, the seasons pass with a riot of colour, with golden grain in the spring, bright yellow sunflowers in summer and snowy white cotton in the early autumn.

The best of Turkey's Aegean coast

The Turkish Aegean offers a wealth of fantastic experiences that fill the hours from just after dawn until well after dusk. To get the most out of your trip, you need to travel backwards in time to the first millennium BC, then zip forward to the best in 21st-century fun. Here are some of the key attractions.

Curetes Street at Ephesus Walk in the footsteps of St Paul down Curetes Street at Ephesus, the most complete ancient city ever excavated in Europe, and a place steeped in atmosphere (page 75).

The bars of Bodrum's old town Chill out in the bars of Bodrum's old town. The Aegean's most sophisticated resort is perfect for a drink overlooking the harbour (page 46).

Get foamed at Halikarnas disco For a wild night out, it does not get more extreme than this (page 46).

Bodrum's castle Explore the ancient underwater finds at Bodrum's castle. Marine archaeology was born here and this museum has some of the best finds in the world (page 38).

Dip your toes in the water on a boat trip There is nothing better to drain the stress from your body than to go on a simple *gület* (traditional wooden boat) journey, sailing around the Aegean coast to hidden coves.

Visit the ancient oracle at Didyma Perhaps you will find out what this week's winning lottery numbers are (page 85)!

Spa at Çesme Cleanse your body with a spa treatment at Çesme. A new you? Well perhaps a revitalized you after a visit to one of these modern therapeutic centres (page 17).

Visit another country – a day trip to Greece Enjoy a few hours consuming *souvlaki* and *retsina*, just a little way off the Turkish coast on the Greek islands of Chios (see page 20) and Samos (see page 33).

Barter for a bargain at the bazaar Shopping is a performance on the Aegean coast – it is theatre, all designed to get you to part with your hard-earned cash.

Pamukkale, the 'cotton castle' One of nature's most awe-inspiring sights, with its glittering white pools of scallop-like hot springs that feature on a hillside (page 78).

RESORTS
Places under the sun

Çeşme
windsurfing and hot springs

Set on the very easternmost tip of the largest peninsula on the Aegean coast, Çeşme (pronounced *Cheshmey*), is a pretty town that has grown around a sturdy Genoese castle and Ottoman kervansaray. To the north and south there are numerous coves with small sandy bays and hills filled with fragrant orange groves.

The steady *ımbat* winds blow across the peninsula all year round, making Çeşme cooler than many Turkish resorts. These winds are ideal for sailing and for the newer sport of windsurfing – so much so that the region plays host to several international windsurfing tournaments throughout the summer season.

Çeşme's other claim to fame is its mineral springs. These have been drawing people here for therapy and pleasure since Roman times. Today its best hotels have high-class spa facilities, but you can still join the locals for free at public hot springs around the town.

Unusually for Turkey, Çeşme is a little short of ancient remains, but you are only a day trip away from several important archaeological sites.

Windsurfing

HISTORY

Before the rise of Izmir (see page 70), Çeşme was the region's major port, and the end of the Silk Road for the camel caravans that crossed central Asia and the Middle East. From here the goods were taken by ship to the cities of the Mediterranean.

The Byzantines gave the town to the Genoese in the 14th century when they could not control the area. It was captured by the Ottomans in the 16th century but continued to have a large Greek Orthodox Christian (old Byzantine) population.

The Greek and Turkish communities lived together in relative peace until the Turkish Republic was founded in the 1920s. The Greek and Turkish governments decided to swap their two communities, so the Greeks here had to resettle on the Greek mainland and Turks born on Greek soil had to move across the Aegean to Turkey.

Today, Çeşme and its surrounding peninsula still have many reminders of Greek life, including distinctive architecture and abandoned churches dotting the hillsides.

THINGS TO SEE & DO

Ayios Haralambos ★

The large 19th-century Greek church of Ayios Haralambos lay empty for many years after the exchange of populations in the 1920s but today the plain, fortress-like building has been restored and reopened as the Emir Caka Art Gallery. It is the region's main cultural and art centre and offers a range of exhibitions throughout the summer. ⓐ İnkilap Caddesi ● Open 09.00–13.00 and 16.00–20.00 ● Admission free

Boat trips ★★★

There are boat trips to isolated beaches and coves all around the peninsula, but one of the most popular is a visit out to Donkey Island. As the name suggests, it is inhabited by numerous donkeys that live wild. They were originally left here when the farmers abandoned the island and moved to the mainland. The donkeys thrived and the island has now been classified as a national park.

Castle ★★

When the Genoese took control of the area in the 14th century they built the original fortress on the hillside overlooking the port. In the 16th century the castle was extended by the Ottomans, but it was destroyed during the wars with Venice in the 17th century. It was rebuilt but lost its strategic value after 1833. It now houses the Çeşme Archaeological Museum with a small but interesting collection of armaments and finds from the area, including some from Erythrai.
Ⓐ On the seafront Ⓒ Open 08.30–17.30 (May–Oct); 08.30–12.30 and 13.30–17.30 (Nov–Apr); closed Mon (winter) ⓘ Admission charge

Kervansaray or Caravanserai ★★

The 16th-century *kervansaray* – a place where the camel trains could rest along the silk route – of Öküz Mehmet Pasa was a gift from Sultan Süleyman the Magnificent. It was built to provide accommodation for travellers taking the journey across to Chios and is still a hotel today, although it has been totally renovated. Wander into the cool courtyard and maybe have some tea while you enjoy the architecture.
Ⓐ Bayazit Caddesi Ⓒ Open 24 hours ⓘ Admission free

Tour of the Drinking Fountains ★

The word Çeşme means 'drinking fountain' in Turkish and the name is derived from the more than 40 fountains and ornate public water sources that once decorated the town. Today there are still over a dozen Seljuk and Ottoman fountains in the streets of the old town – you can sometimes pick up a simple map from the tourist office (Ⓐ İşkele Meydani 8 – in the main square of the town Ⓣ 0232 712 6653) that leads you to them.

Diving ★★

Diving is taking off in the area. **Dolphin Land** (Ⓐ Dalyankoy Limani Ⓣ 0232 337 0161 Ⓦ www.divecesme.com) offers PADI training and accompanied dives for both beginners and qualified divers and has over 20 dive sites around the peninsula.

FISHING PORT
AEGEAN SEA
DALYAN & AYAYORGI BEACH
IZMIR, ILICA, ŞIFNE & ERYTHRAI
İNKILAP CADDESİ
AYIOS HARALAMBOS / EMIR CAKA ART GALLERY
TAXI RANK
CASTLE
MARAŞ SOKAK
FERRY TO CHIOS
İSKELE MEYDANI
CUSTOMS OFFICE
DOLMUSES TO ALAÇATİ, ALTINKUM & ILICA
KERVANSARAY
KALE SOKAK
BELEDIYE HAMAMI
ÇARŞI CADDESİ
BEYAZIT CADDESİ
MÜFTÜ SOKAK
N
0
250
500 m
0
0.25 mile
ALTINKUM PIRLANTA BEACH
TURGUT ÖZAL CADDESİ
ALAÇATİ

Windsurfing ★★★

B&G Surf This is the place to go for instruction and board rental. You can start from scratch or take one-to-one improver courses. The surf school is owned by a Turkish national windsurf champion and a sports educator. ⓐ Alaçatı Beach ⓣ 0232 716 6605 ⓦ www.bgsurfokolu.com

Club Mistral This company, based in Germany, has wind and kite-surfing training centres across the globe, with English-speaking instructors. ⓐ Alaçatı, near Cesme ⓣ 00 49 881 909 6010 ⓦ www.clubmistral.com

Kite surfing ★★★

The centre of Turkish kitesurfing is based at Pirlanta beach which benefits from the prevailing Aegean winds and has hosted national and international championships. The **kitesurfing school** (ⓐ Pirlanta Plaji Ciftlik Koy ⓣ 0536 458 8494 ⓦ www.kitesurfbeach.com) at the beach is the best in Turkey and you can take beginners' courses or rent equipment.

SHOPPING

İnkilap Caddesi, Çeşme's main street, is the centre for shopping and nightlife. There is a full range of souvenir shops here, from inexpensive to pricey, and it is traffic free, so you can stroll to your heart's content – that is, if the shopkeepers do not grab your attention.

One unique souvenir to look out for here is food flavoured with mastic (*sakız* in Turkish). The Çeşme peninsula is the only place in Turkey where this aromatic resin is harvested. The Ottomans used it as a breath freshener and flavouring. Local growers produce mastic jam, mastic ice cream and also mastic *rakı* (a strong spirit similar to vodka) by infusing the resin in the alcohol.

Spas & Turkish baths ★★

Çeşme is famous for its natural hot springs, renowned since antiquity for their health-giving properties. The water temperature is 55°C (131°F) and contains sodium chloride, magnesium sulphate and calcium bicarbonate. The mineral-rich water is relaxing and said to cure various ailments.

Belediye Hamamı A genuine old bathhouse that offers mixed sessions several times per week. ⓐ Near the *kervansaray* Ⓛ Open 08.00–22.00

Thermalife Natural Spa This 7869 sq m (25,800 sq ft) spa center includes an indoor seawater pool, sauna, steam room, thalassotherapy jet and affusion showers, physiotherapy area, fitness centre and beauty salon. Treatments include hydrating moss or mud body wrap, and pressotherapy, a rejuvenating full-body lymphatic drainage massage, plus a full range of aromatherapy and massage treatments to reduce stress, eliminate toxins and increase metabolism. If you don't want a treatment, you can just take a swim in the natural thermal pools. This is the most luxurious place for a swim, but it is also the most expensive. ⓐ Sheraton Çeşme Hotel Resort & Spa, Şifne Caddesi 35, Ilıca ⓣ 0232 723 1240 ⓦ www.starwood.com

Yildiz The Yildiz peninsula thermal spring is popular with local families. The temperature of the water reaches 60°C (140°F), but it emerges into cooler seawater already in the rocky natural pool. ⓐ West of Ilica town ❗ Admission free

The Spavit Center This place offers medical therapies and a full range of relaxing and well-being treatments such as reflexology, facials and massage. There is also a sports centre, hot mineral springs and a *hammam*. ⓐ Süzer Paradise Limani Merkii, Çark Plaji, right on the beach ⓣ 0232 716 9774 ⓔ spavit@suzerparadise.com

BEACHES

Tekke Beach ★

The town beach is not the best one around the resort, but it is the perfect place to cool down after a morning's shopping. ⓐ Just north of the port in Çeşme

Ilıca ★★★

The primary beach area of Ilıca (Uluja) and the adjoining bay of Şifne (Shifni) have long, fine strands that are some of the best in the Aegean. The warm shallows of Şifne extend over 100 m (109 yd) out into the water. The Romans used to come here to enjoy the therapeutic springs, and today there are some excellent international five-star hotels here, offering a luxury that is not always available in the other major resorts. ⓐ 2 km (1 mile) from Çeşme

White sand beaches stretch for miles along the coastline

Ayayorgi Beach ★★

A secluded bay hidden among fragrant orange groves. There is no sand here, which is not ideal for young children. Instead you enter the sea via cement lidos. The waters here are exceptionally clear, so if you like snorkelling it is ideal. You can also rent kayaks and paddleboats to explore the rocky shoreline. ⓐ 3 km (2 miles) north of Çeşme; there is no public transport, so you will need to take a taxi or hire a car

Altınkum Beach ★★★

Çeşme's 'Golden Beach' offers several long, unspoilt golden sand bays that rival Ilıca as the best in the northern Aegean. There is far less development here but still a selection of cafés for refreshment. ⓐ 9 km (5 miles) south of the town; there are regular *dolmuş* services from the bus station at Çeşme

Pirlanta Beach ★★

Pirlanta or 'Diamond Beach', is named after the brilliant, almost white sand that twinkles in the sunshine (sunglasses are advised). ⓐ Closer to the town, by a couple of kilometres, than Altınkum

EXCURSIONS

Erythrai ★

The Çeşme peninsula has the least amount of ancient remains along the Aegean coast, but there is one small site. Erythrai was the site of a renowned Sybil, or prophetess, and also had a temple containing a statue of Hercules.

Most of the stone has been recycled for later buildings, so there is not much to see. Some sections of what must have been a vast outer wall are still standing, and there is a Roman villa and a Hellenistic (late-Greek) mosaic floor. Statues, jewellery and other finds from the city are on show in the Archaeological Museum at Izmir (see page 70).

Because the area has been declared a national heritage site by the Turkish authorities, the modern village of Ildıri on the site cannot be

expanded and is semi-abandoned. The Acropolis at the top of the site offers wonderful views across the small islands of the Aegean, especially at sunset. ⓐ 20 km (12 miles) north-east of Çeşme

Alaçatı ★★★

Alaçatı is a wonderful old town with some excellent, 19th-century Greek mansions surrounded by a verdant landscape of orange and olive groves plus the only mastic orchards in Turkey.

A collection of old windmills lines the hillside, and some have been converted into good restaurants and cafés. They do not work, but their presence gives an indication of the strength of the winds that blow down the Aegean across the peninsula. Today these year-round high winds (and shallow water) help to make the beach at Alaçati, one of the top three windsurfing destinations in the world. ⓐ Located 9 km (6 miles) south-east of Çeşme; the beach is 4 km (2.5 miles) from town

---

Ertürk Agency organizes a range of activities and trips on the surrounding Çeşme peninsula. ⓐ Beyazit Caddesi 7 ⓣ 0232 712 6768

Chios (Hios) ★★

You will find the Greek island of Chios delightfully free of visitors because it is one of the least 'touristy' islands in the Aegean. The capital of the island, Chios Town, is one of the least attractive towns in the Greek Aegean, but it has a fine castle and archaeological museum. It is best to rent a car or agree a rate with a taxi to tour the island's other attractions.

Chios has made a living out of mastic for centuries and the mastic villages (*mastihohoria*) inland boast some grand Genoese mansions built in the 14th and 15th centuries, set among a glorious verdant countryside. Pyrgi village is unique because of its distinctive decoration. The walls of all the houses are covered with black and white geometric patterns called *xysta*. It is also worth visiting Nea Moni, one of the most beautiful religious sites in the Aegean. Founded in 1049, the church has some exceptional Byzantine mosaics. There are daily trips (weather permitting) from the harbour, and commercial ferries from the new harbour.

RESTAURANTS (see map on page 15)

Bize Bize € ❶ Authentic, inexpensive Turkish snacks at this tiny establishment that specializes in *İskender* and *döner kebabs*. A great place for hungry tums at lunchtime or during a shopping trip. ⓐ İnkılap Caddesi 6 ⓒ Open 08.00–01.00

Escueto €€ ❷ One of the hippest places in town, Escueto serves tasty Mexican, Spanish and Tex-Mex dishes, including reasonable tapas. They import a lot of ingredients to ensure an authentic flavour. They also do a great line in frozen cocktails – try the margarita – and offer genuine tequila. ⓐ İnkılap Caddesi 8 ⓣ 0232 712 0696 ⓒ Open 08.00–02.00

Hasan Usta Süt Tatlılari € ❸ The best place in Çeşme to try delicious milk puddings. It's not a fancy place but it's very authentic. You'll find Turkish families there finishing off their evenings and it gets very busy at the weekend in summer. ⓐ Cumhuriyet Meydani 12 ⓒ Open 08.00–midnight

Kale Lokantesi € ❹ One of the best places in the Aegean to try good home-cooked Turkish dishes in an authentic *lokanta*. It has a rustic interior but the food is excellent, and great value for money. There is no menu, just a small choice of traditional dishes (whatever is fresh and in season). They also do a tasty *döner kebab*. Not surprisingly, Kale gets very busy with locals and you will not go wrong if you follow their lead. ⓐ Kervansaray yani 11, Çarşi Caddesi ⓣ 0232 712 0519 ⓒ Open 09.00–midnight

Körfez €€ ❺ A more upmarket option than the Kale, Körfez overlooks the harbour and serves a range of locally caught fish. If you are more adventurous you could choose one of the more classic Ottoman style dishes cooked on an *ocakbasi*, or open grill.
ⓐ Yali Caddesi 12 ⓣ 0232 712 6718 Ⓛ Open daily noon–midnight

Restoran Imren €€€ ❻ This is a place to treat yourself to something a little more upscale with slightly more formal service but still with that classic Turkish welcome. Eat outside on the terrace.
ⓐ İnkılap Caddesi 6 ⓣ 0232 712 7620

Restoran Patika €–€€€ ❼ A converted town house now makes a pretty restaurant with a vast menu and prices to suit every pocket. There's live music every evening in the summer. ⓐ Cumhuriyet Meydani (left of the Belediye or Town Hall) ⓣ 0232 712 6357. Open daily 11.00–midnight

Rumeli Pastanesi € ❽ Turks flock to this shop for the very best homemade ice-cream, including a mastic flavour which is unique to this area. It's a good option to finish your meal. ⓐ İnkılap Caddesi 44 Open daily 09.00–midnight

NIGHTLIFE

Felix Roof Bar ❾ At the top of the 5-star Sheraton Hotel, this bar is one of the most sophisticated and expensive in the northern Aegean. The surroundings are luxurious and offer long-range views across the bay. There's live music nightly. ⓐ Sheraton Çeşme Hotel, Şifne Caddesi 35, Ilıca ⓣ 0232 723 1240 Open 16.00–02.00

SkyBar ❿ As the name suggests, this rooftop bar offers great views across the town and picks up the breezes that skim across the peninsula. There's always a crowd in the evenings. ⓐ Cumhuriyet Meydani Open 11.00–03.00

Wine Plaza ⓫ This is the latest hip place to be in Çeşme, contained in an old Greek mansion that has been beautifully transformed into a sophisticated wine bar. The food on offer is Italian style but this is more of an after-dinner spot. Enjoy a glass of wine out on the terrace – there's a good range of Turkish options for you to try – or come after 22.30 Wed–Sat to enjoy live music. ⓐ İnkılap Caddesi 27 ⓣ 0232 712 095 Open noon–03.00

The buzzing nightlife continues late into the evening

Altınkum
British family favourite

Altınkum (pronounced Altunkum) has developed fast since the early 1980s. The long 'golden beach' that gives the resort its name is its claim to fame and the three bays along the coastline have everything both children and adults need for holiday fun. This resort is a favourite with many UK tourists, with a range of 'roast beef dinner' restaurants and re-runs of favourite TV comedy shows or live football matches in the bars. As a result, hundreds of Britons have bought apartments here in the last few years. From here it is an easy excursion ride to the best the Aegean area has to offer. If you want a good beach resort with more than a few reminders of home, this is the place for you.

THINGS TO SEE & DO

Boat trips ★★

Most tour boats will take you on the 'five-island' tour, though few actually stop at any island. Swimming and snorkelling is from the boat.

BEACHES

The busiest beach, **First Beach** sits directly in front of the heart of town and has access to most cafés, bars and a good range of water sports. It does get very crowded in high season. **Second Beach** is a little less developed, and for the most peace and quiet (just a couple of cafés and lots of free sand), head to **Third Beach**, where you also have the best snorkelling.

EXCURSIONS

Didyma ★★★

The ancient temple site at Didyma (see page 85) is only 5 km (3 miles) north of the resort at the village of Didim.

Bodrum by boat ★★★

There is a daily ferry to Bodrum (see page 52) during the summer, where you can sample a little Turkish sophistication.

The golden sands of Altinkum's bay

RESTAURANTS

Alo 24 € The best place in town for an inexpensive lunch or snacks throughout the day – Alo 24 turns out tons of *pide* and *döner kebabs*. It is a really inexpensive place for children to fill up after an action-packed day on the beach. ⓐ Atatürk Bul, Opposite GIMA Supermarket ⓑ Open 07.00–23.00

A Touch of Class €€ An unassuming restaurant that has been in business for 15 years while its more glamorous neighbours have come and gone, A Touch of Class offers good Turkish food and adds entertainment such as karaoke and Turkish nights into the mix. There is a good-value set meal. ⓐ Yali Caddesi Goçler Mevkii 129, Altinkum ⓣ 0256 813 1168 ⓑ Open 07.00–midnight

Janibo's €€ English-owned restaurant with a huge garden that serves a genuine English breakfast and UK favourites throughout the day, including scones and cream and trifle. There are sports channels on the big screen and a free pool. ⓐ Karakol Caddesi No. 4, Altinkum ⓣ 0256 813 4302 ⓑ Open 07.00–02.00

Pinocchio's €€ With a dining terrace on the seafront on First Beach, Pinocchio's has a great setting. The menu is Turkish/English (including traditional Sunday lunch and freshly baked bread and cakes) with a trained management team and an attention to detail that others do not always have. Live entertainment. ⓐ Yali Caddesi 71, First Beach, Altinkum ⓣ 0256 813 1215 ⓑ Open 08.00–02.00

NIGHTLIFE

British Pub Opened in 1997, British Pub does exactly what it says on the tin and has a loyal band of annual regulars. ⓐ Yali Caddesi 123, Altinkum ⓑ Open 08.00–03.00

Ege Bar A long-standing favourite for the last few years, Ege has entertaining staff and dancers, but is also a great place to chill in the early evenings. ⓐ Dolphin Square ⓑ Open 11.00–03.00

Medusa Nightclub The largest venue and only real club in Altinkum has great chart and Turkish pop music. It is open air, so you can enjoy the stars while you dance. You may need to queue to get in during peak season. ⓐ Yali Konagi Caddesi, Altinkum ⓑ Open 21.00–04.00 (June–early Sept) ⓘ Entrance fee includes first drink

Ancient ruins of Didyma

Kuşadası
Aegean 'mega-resort'

Kuşadası (pronounced Kushadaser) is a vast and seemingly ever-expanding holiday town. It is probably Turkey's most versatile resort, with a huge selection of hotels, apartments, restaurants and bars for package tourists, one of the largest marinas along the coast for the yachting crowd and a huge cruise port for passengers on the Aegean tour who disembark in the morning to visit Ephesus (see page 73) and get whisked away to their next port of call in Greece – usually sailing before nightfall.

The heart of Kuşadası is a tiny old town with a maze of narrow alleyways planned and built during Ottoman times. You will find some of the best shopping and nightlife in Turkey here, with top-quality jewellery, leather and carpet shops tempting the cruise-ship crowd, mass-produced designer fakes, plus a huge selection of bars and clubs with a young, boisterous and mainly British crowd.

Today 'holidayland' stretches over several kilometres of coastline. It cannot be described as attractive, with the hills covered with a jungle of white-painted concrete, but for 'party central' look no further.

HISTORY

No one knows exactly when the site was first settled, but the nearby ancient city of Panionian was the annual meeting place of the Ionian League in the first millennium BC. When the port of Ephesus dried up in the 6th and 7th centuries, Kuşadası took over and became an important trade centre run by Venetian and Genovese merchants. They built the fortress to guard the port.

In the 16th century the Ottomans arrived and Kuşadası was reinvented by Öküz Mehmet Pasa, grand vizier to a couple of Ottoman sultans. He built the *kervansaray*, expanded the fortress and chose to call the town Kuşadası, or 'Bird Island', a name taken from the tiny island situated just offshore.

 Tourist office ⓐ Liman Caddesi 13 across from the port entrance ⓣ 0256 614 1103

THINGS TO SEE & DO

Güvercin Adası ★★

Bird Island was renamed Güvercin Adası, or 'Pigeon Island', and today it is connected to the mainland by a pedestrian causeway that acts as a dock for small excursion boats. The shady terraced area around the fortifications has relaxing tea gardens and cafés and offers lovely views at sunset and across the seafront and cruise port. ⓐ On the waterfront ◷ Castle 08.00–17.30 (Tues–Sun), closed Mon ⓘ Admission charge

Öküz Mehmet Pasa Kervansaray ★★

Wander into the cool courtyard of this 16th-century *kervansaray* – a sort of guest house/hotel where you could also rest your animals – that has been welcoming guests for over 300 years. Today the architecture remains authentic although the rooms have all the mod cons. There is a good carpet shop here (expensive) and the hotel holds regular 'Turkish evenings' (see Excursions, page 58). Atatürk Bul 0256 614 4155 Open 24 hours Admission free, with charge for Turkish night

Adaland Waterpark ★★★

Some 25 acres (10 ha) of parkland with 20 rides, including Kamikaze, a 52 m (171 ft) drop, children's pool, ring rides and water slides. The park also includes water disco, a bowling alley and beach volleyball. Bars serve alcohol as well as soft drinks. Çam Limanı, 5 km (3 miles) north of Kuşadası 0256 618 1252 www.adaland.com Open 09.00–18.00, longer in Jul–Aug, closed Nov–Apr

Aqualand ★★★

Some 70,000 sq m (76,580 sq yd) of pools, rides and slides, plus a range of seagoing watersports equipment on the beach. Sahil Sitelleri, Long Beach 0256 618 1252 www.aqualand-kusadasi.com Open 09.00–18.00, longer in Jul–Aug, closed Nov–Apr

Aquafantasy Waterpark ★★★

The largest water park in Turkey, Aquafantasy has some of the highest energy rides, including the 'Castle' – three interloping slides of 120 m (131 ft) – and 'Proracer', the only head-down ride in Turkey with four lanes for slide racing. It also features a pool with ten different types of wave, plus 'Treasure Island', an area specifically for young children.
No alcohol is served here. Ephesus Beach, Pamuçak 0232 839 111 Open 09.00–18.00, longer in Jul–Aug, closed Nov–Apr

Water sports ★★★

Blue Sky Water Sports Has an excellent beach sports and water sports centre with jet skis, parasailing, water rides like bananas, water skis and sea kayaks. The Grand Blue Sky Resort just north of Ladies Beach 0256 613 1203 Open 09.00–19.00

KoruMar Hotel A five-star hotel 2 km (1 mile) north of the town with a full range of water sports, water rides and activities. Gazi Begandi Mevkii 0256 618 1530 www.koromarhotel.com.tr Open 09.00–19.00

❶ There is a charge for non-guests for entrance to the beach, in addition to equipment rental

Diving ★★

Seahorse Diving Offers PADI training and guided dive tours for qualified visitors. ⓐ Klaus Murr. Adil Caylan, Deniz Güleç Sokak 1/A and at the Hotel Zinos ⓣ 0256 614 3561 ⓦ www.seahorse-divingkusadasi-tr.com

Aquaventure Diving Centre This centre offers several dive sites and courses at all levels. ⓐ Adjacent to Blue Sky Water Sports, at the Grand Blue Sky Resort ⓣ 0256 612 8330

Spas & Turkish Baths ★★

Both the baths listed here cater to tourists with mixed male and female sessions – check on times of these sessions beforehand.

Belediye Hamamı ⓐ Sağlik Caddesi ⓣ 0256 614 1219 ◷ 08.00–20.00

Kaleici Hamamı ⓐ Eyül Sokak 7 Kaleiçi ⓣ 0256 614 1292 ◷ 08.00–20.00

BEACHES

Kustur Beach ★★

Kustur is a little over a kilometre of fine sand that has been developed since the 1990s. Because it is a new, pre-planned area, there is an excellent range of cafés and restaurants plus a good choice of water

There's a string of famous beaches to enjoy

sports. The sea often gets rougher in the afternoon as the winds down the Aegean get stronger. ⓐ 6 km (4 miles) north of Kuşadası

Pamuçak Beach ★★

This long, wide beach is an excellent stretch of sand and contains the **Aquafantasy Waterpark**. The southern end is developed, with some large hotel complexes, but you can still escape the crowds if you walk along towards where the River Menderes meets the sea. Some facilities, but not as organized as Ladies Beach. ⓐ 10 km (6 miles) north of the town

Ladies Beach ★★

Kuşadası's most famous beach, this kilometre-long sandy stretch is the heart and soul of holiday fun. Backed by hotels with an excellent range of bars and eateries close by, it also has a full range of facilties, including a good range of water sports. This is the place to be for the young crowd; it does get very busy in high season, so arrive early to get a sunbed. ⓐ A couple of kilometres south of the town centre

Snake Beach ★

Just to the left of Pigeon Island, Snake Beach covers two sides of a small peninsula. Sunbeds and umbrellas and a couple of cafés for snacks, but no water sports. ⓐ 10 minutes' walk from the town centre

Long Beach ★★

As the name suggests, Long Beach is the longest in the Kuşadası region, at 6 km (4 miles). It is now backed by a number of hotels and pensions, so you'll find good water sports at **Aqualand Waterpark**, and range of cafés, bars and restaurants. ⓐ South of the town

Barbaros Beach ★

Barbaros is popular with local families and is usually only packed at weekends. A good, sandy stretch, it is quieter than Ladies Beach, with fewer cafés and bars. ⓐ Only five minutes' south of Ladies Beach on foot

SHOPPING

Kuşadası has the biggest range of shopping in the Aegean, with a great choice in all price ranges, but it also has some of the most persistent salesmen in the business.

You will find the upmarket shops clustered on the seafront (Atatürk Bul) and around the old *kervansaray*. These air-conditioned emporia stock huge silk carpets, Chanel, Prada and Dolce and Gabbana jewellery, plus the biggest diamonds you have ever seen. Quality does not come cheap, but you will pay less than for the genuine article at home.

Kuşadası is also famed for its designer rip-offs, some of them of very good quality. Whatever is in fashion at home, you will find a less expensive fake version here. Although the narrow streets have plenty of shops you will find the greatest choice at the main bazaar. This is a very touristy market and the sales patter is constant, but you can pick up excellent bargains including watches, sunglasses, bags and clothing. The bazaar is also a great place to buy leather goods (bags, jackets and trousers) and to stock up on socks and underwear.

The Friday market (opposite the main bus station) is the place where the farmers of the region bring their crops for sale. It is a really bustling, atmospheric place.

In Kuşadası you will find lots of souvenirs priced in pounds, so do not change all your spending money into Turkish Lira.

EXCURSIONS

Dilek National Park ★★

A rocky finger of land pointing out into the Aegean, the Dilek Peninsula is one of a largest remaining swathes of unspoilt pine forest left along the Aegean coast. Its strategic position close to the Greek island of Samos saved it from development because it was off limits to all but

the Turkish military. Today, they still have a base at the western end but the rest, now a national park, is a great place to come and get away from the crowds.

The small, sandy coves and crystal-clear waters are perfect for sunbathing, swimming and snorkelling. They line the northern shore and get quieter the further away you get from the ticket office – from Içmeler Köyü, the most crowded and with café and picnic tables, to Karasu Köyü, a pebble beach with views out to Samos.

Dilek is also a great place for walking and hiking (be prepared with water, snacks and proper clothing). The park protects several species of rare animals including, it is said, a small population of lynx (wild cats).
Dilek Park ⓐ 30 km (19 miles) south of Kuşadası; take a *dolmuş* (bus) from Kuşadası to the first beach, but your own transport is more practical for touring the whole park ◔ Open 08.00–18.30 ❶ Admission charge

Samos ★

The Greek Island of Samos, located 3 km (2 miles) off the Turkish coastline just south of Kuşadası, has taken a back seat in Aegean history since its 'golden age' in the 5th century BC and today is known mostly for its vast pine forests. The capital, Samos Town, or Bathy, on the north coast, has a fine harbour-front promenade, but the smaller town of Pithagorio on the south coast makes a better excursion.

An ancient capital during the reign of the powerful ruler Polycrates in the 5th century BC (he had storyteller Aesop and mathematician Pythagoras in his court), Pithagorio has a picturesque harbour and ancient remains. In the hills above is perhaps the most amazing example of Polycrates' wealth and power. He funded the cutting of a tunnel over 1000 m (1094 yds) long through the hill to bring water to the capital. The Tunnel of Eupalinos can be explored, but it is not for the claustrophobic.

To the west, beyond the airport, are the remains of the Temple of Hera, or the Heraion. It would have been the largest in the world at the time, but it was never completed. ⓐ Daily trips (weather permitting early and late in the season) take place from Kuşadası harbour.

RESTAURANTS (see map on page 28)

Avlu € ❶ Always popular with local Turks, this traditional *lokanta* has no menu but serves a range of good, basic hearty food. Head into the kitchen to see what looks tasty, but try the succulent lamb stew with pilaf rice if you can. Ⓐ Barbaros Hayrattin Caddesi (just before the post office) Ⓣ 0256 614 7995 Ⓛ Open 08.00–midnight

Çam €€ ❷ Overlooking the fishing port, it is not surprising that this restaurant serves a good range of excellent fresh seafood. The decor is basic, but the restaurant has a very good reputation. Ⓐ Balıkçı Limanı Ⓣ 0256 614 1051 Ⓛ Open 11.00–midnight

Captain's House €€ ❸ A wonderful, renovated mansion houses this renowned fish restaurant and bar, which has an excellent reputation with locals and visitors looking for somewhere upmarket to eat. Lovely terrace. Ⓐ Atatürk Bul 66 Ⓣ 0256 612 1200 Ⓛ Open 11.00–02.00 ❗ Make reservations in high season

Holiday Inn €–€€ ❹ This oddly named restaurant has a strong reputation for excellent Turkish food and tasty grills, with huge portions at not too expensive prices. Ⓐ Kahramanlar Caddesi Ⓣ 0252 612 8940 Ⓛ Open 08.00–midnight

Istanbul Meyhanesi €€ ❺ A perfect example of a typical Turkish tavern, Istanbul Meyhanesi serves simple traditional *meze* dishes along with copious amounts of beer or *raki*. You will find yourself surrounded by groups of friendly locals most evenings and weekends, when it gets really busy and noisy. Ⓐ Kişla Sokak 7 Ⓣ 0256 613 1677 Ⓛ Open 19.00–02.00 ❗ Book a table at weekends

Kazım Usta €€ ❻ The seafood here is excellent, and Turks also come for the extensive and delicious *meze* selection. Ⓐ Balıkcı Limanı, on the harbour front Ⓣ 0256 614 1226 Ⓛ Open noon–midnight

Dining at the beautiful floodlit marina

Öz Urfa € ⑦ Good, clean kebab place that has been in business for ages. Öz Urfa has the advantage that it is licensed, so you can get beer or wine with your meal. Cephane Sokak 9 0252 614 6070 Open 08.00–midnight

Paşa Restaurant €–€€ ⑧ This family-run restaurant has tables set out in the pretty courtyard of an old Greek mansion. The menu concentrates on standard *meze*, grills and kebabs, for which they have a good reputation, plus a small selection of seafood. Cephane Sokak 21 0252 612 3133 Open 11.00–midnight

NIGHTLIFE

Kuşadası's nightlife is the loudest and most energetic in the Aegean and much of it is found in the old town, in the narrow streets bordered by Barbaros Hayrettin Caddesi and Saglik Sokak. It is said that Kuşadası's Barlar Sokagi (walk up Barbaros Hayrettin Caddesi, turn right onto Saglik

Sokak, and then left under the arch) boasts more Irish pubs per square inch than Dublin. Although this must be an exaggeration, it tells you what to expect – lots of bars and discos competing for your money. Bar crawling seems to be the norm, but here are a few places you might want to try:

Club Kervansaray ❾ One of the best places in the Aegean to enjoy a Turkish night folklore show. The genuine Ottoman *kervansaray* sets the scene with its architecture, and the show takes place in the central courtyard. The food is of a reasonable quality and it is an entertaining evening. ⓐ Atatürk Bul 2 ⓣ 0256 614 4115 ❗ Performances nightly at 21.00 hours in peak season – drops to two or three times a week early or late in season

Ecstacy ❿ Kuşadası's major nightclub is a massive open-air arena that tends to stick mainly to the latest top 40 dance tunes. This is the venue where you can finish your evening after a few drinks in the bars earlier on. ⓐ Kaleiçi Sakarya 10 ⓣ 0256 612 2208 ⓛ Open 21.00–04.00

Jimmy's Bar ⓫ Long-standing Irish-style bar with energetic staff and loud music from the 1970s through to today. Jimmy's shows Premiership football matches on large-screen TVs so you will not miss too much soccer while you are relaxing. ⓐ Barler Sokak ⓣ 0256 612 1318 ⓛ Open 11.00–04.00

Orient Bar ⓬ A long-standing favourite, Orient Bar is a rather laid-back place. It is the bar to visit for chilling out over drinks rather than a high-energy place, and live music is played there on most nights. ⓐ Camikebir Mah, Kaleiçi Sakarya ⓣ 0256 612 8838 ⓛ Open 11.00–02.00

Taps ⓭ English-owned pub/bar that is popular with tourists and ex-pats who want a little touch of home. It is a good place to catch up with fellow Brits. ⓐ Kaleiçi Sakarya ⓣ 0256 612 1317 ⓛ Open 08.00–03.00

Bodrum
Ibiza meets St Tropez

Turkey's oldest tourist resort, the fishing community of Bodrum was adopted by the Turkish artistic community in the 1920s. It continues to attract an upmarket Turkish clientele who head out of Istanbul or Ankara during the summer. Bodrum was discovered by European holidaymakers in the 1980s, but refused to bow to the pressure to 'build 'em high and build 'em quick' that has spoiled some resorts, and passed laws to restrict building size and design. It has retained its authentic character and is perhaps the prettiest resort in the Aegean and one of the most attractive in Turkey.

The town has many attractions and caters to many different types of visitor. It is popular with the yachting crowd, who moor up in the large harbour and frequent the waterfront bars and restaurants. It is a great place to be young and fashionable, rivalling the Mediterranean hot spots of Ibiza in Spain and Mykonos in Greece. Bodrum also has the best range of shopping and dining in the Aegean, with something good to suit every pocket.

Bodrum castle overlooking the marina

Staying in Bodrum will not suit everyone, however. Most town hotels are small and traditional rather than large 'resort' establishments with lots of activities. Also, one thing that the resort lacks is a good beach. The town beach is narrow, crowded and not very attractive. Families and 'bronzers' would be better making a base at one of Bodrum's close satellite resorts such as Gümbet (see page 48) or Bitez (see page 53). From both these places you can take a short *dolmuş* (mini-bus) trip into Bodrum – in summer these operate almost 24 hours a day – to sample its sophisticated and cosmopolitan atmosphere.

HISTORY

The town was once the ancient city of Halicarnassus, home to the Carian people. The most famous Carian ruler, King Mausolus (*c.* 377–353 BC), built himself a monumental tomb known as the Mausoleum that became one of the 'seven wonders of the ancient world'. The Knights of St John made Bodrum their home after they were ousted from Jerusalem, but they had to leave when the Ottomans arrived in the area in the 14th century.

THINGS TO SEE & DO

Castle of St Peter (the Petronium) ★★★

This is one of the finest and most complete castles in Turkey, built by the crusading Knights of St John in 1408. The building alone, with its dungeon and towers, would make it worth a visit, but the castle is also home to the Museum of Underwater Archaeology (see below) displaying unique collections of ancient artefacts. There are superb views across Bodrum and the sea from the extensive walls and parapets, and you can enjoy a glass of wine in the bar in the English Tower. ⓐ On the harbour front ⓣ 0252 316 2516 ◷ Open 08.30–noon and 13.00–17.30 (Tues–Sun), closed Mon; some parts of the museum open at different hours (see page 40) ❶ Admission charge

Museum of Underwater Archaeology ★★★

Opened in 1963, several of the halls of the castle have been skilfully refurbished to display the most important collection of ancient

GÜMBET
BODRUM PENINSULA
DEDEMAN AQUA PARK
MOSQUE
CAFER PAŞA SOKAK
ANCIENT AMPHITHEATRE
KIBRIS SEHITLER CADDESI (RING ROAD)
AEGEAN SEA
Yacht Marina
Tepecık
Salmakis Bay
MOSQUE
MAUSOLEUM
West Harbour
NEYZEN TEVFIK CADDESI
Ferry Dock
DIVE AND DAY BOAT TRIPS
SU HOTEL
TURGUT REIS CADDESI
CASTLE OF ST PETER
DIVE AND DAY BOAT TRIPS
GELENCE SOKAK
BELEDIYE MEYDANI
ISKELE MEYDANI
KALE CADDESI
MUSEUM OF UNDERWATER ARCHAEOLOGY
MOSQUE
MOSQUE
TURKKUYUSU CADDESI
Kumbahçe Bay
ÇEVAT SAKIR CADDESI
N
DR. ALIM BEY CADDESI
WEEKLY MARKET PLACE
ARTEMIS CADDESI
500 m
UÇKUYULAR CADDESI
ATATÜRK CADDESI
DERE UMURCA SOKAK
(BAR STREET)
MHURIYET CADDESI
ZEKI MUREN CADDESI
MUMTAZ ATAMAN CADDESI
İÇMELER
MILAS & AIRPORT

underwater finds in Europe, discovered mainly in nearby waters. Exhibits range from the contents of ships and ship reconstructions, to arrangements of artefacts showing how they were grouped on board ship:

Ulu Burun Finds

The most important collection is the amazing early finds dating from the Late Bronze Age (1300–1600 BC) that show just how important sea trade was to our ancient ancestors. The world's oldest known shipwreck, the *Ulu Burun*, found in 1982, is fascinating. Excavated finds include gold jewellery from Ancient Egypt, elephant and hippopotamus ivory from central Africa, Mycenaean swords, Syrian pottery, valuable copper ingots probably picked up in Cyprus, thought to have been the copper capital of the ancient world, and many other artefacts.

East Roman Ship

Set in the chapel, the East Roman Ship dates from the 7th century AD and offers a full-scale reconstruction of part of the ship and the excavation site.

The Glass Wreck

Archaeologists assume that the 'glass wreck' ship was carrying a cargo of broken glass because the amount of damage to the glass items found was so extensive. Today they lie in huge piles, with some identifiable items in cases. Academics are most excited about the early Islamic glass found here. Open 09.00–noon and 14.00–16.00 (Tues–Fri) Extra admission charge

The Carian Princess Room or Ada Hall

The exhibits here belonged to a local princess, one of the ruling family of this region during Hellenistic times (323–31 BC). The ornate tomb and selection of gold jewellery hint at a very pampered life. Open 09.00–noon and 14.00–16.00 (Tues–Fri) Separate admission charge

Mausoleum ★

The site of Mausolus' tomb is a bit of a disappointment. The Knights of St John recycled the stone for their castle during the early 15th century so there is little to see. ⓐ Turgut Reis Caddesi (above the town), signposted from the Neyzen Tefvik Caddesi ⓣ 0252 316 1219 ◷ Open 08.30–noon and 13.00–17.00, closed Mon ⓘ Admission charge

Diving ★★★

There is excellent diving all around the Bodrum coast and this is one of the best places in the eastern Mediterranean to learn to dive.

Aegean Pro Dive Center Provides PADI certification, three- and five-day packages, plus snorkelling for non-divers. ⓐ Neyzen Tevfik Caddesi 212 ⓣ 0252 316 0737/313 1296 ⓦ www.aegeanprodive.com ◷ Open Apr–Oct

Poseidon Diving Systems This is one of the best of several companies that offer day trips for those who are already qualified, with a diving com-panion, equipment and private transportation. ⓐ Neyzen Tevfik Caddesi 80/A ⓣ 0252 313 8727

Dedeman Aqua Park ★

This has a range of rides and pools. ⓐ Kavakali Sarnia Caddesi Sokak 1 (on the road to Ortakent) at the Dedeman Hotel ⓣ 0252 313 8500 ◷ Open 10.00–18.00, closed Nov–Apr ⓘ Admission charge

Birdwatching ★

The Su Hotel offers guided walks in the countryside around Bodrum and guided birdwatching throughout the year. ⓐ Turgutreis Caddesi 1202 ⓣ 0252 316 6906 ⓘ Admission charge; pre-booking essential

The Blue Voyage ★★★

In the 1920s Turkish writer and native of Bodrum Cevat șakir Kabaağaçlı's wrote *Mavi Yolculuk* (*Blue Voyage*) about a simple *gület* (traditional wooden boat) journey from Bodrum around the Lycian coast to the south, capturing the imagination of a generation of Turks. The journey described in *Blue Voyage* takes several days, but follow in Kabaağaçlı's

SHOPPING

Bodrum has probably the best range of shopping in the Aegean. Hip and chic boutiques sit side by side with antique shops, genuine designer names try to attract the yachting set, while market stalls sell rip-offs at a fraction of the price.

Wandering along the streets of the old town – explore the narrow alleyways off **Cumhuriyet Caddesi** and **Dr Alim Bey Caddesi** – is the prefect way to spend a few Turkish Lira and exercise the credit cards. Around the main yacht basin there are some excellent modern boutiques with prices on a par with those at home.

There is a craft market on Tuesdays in Bodrum, and Friday is the day for the produce market.

footsteps by taking a day trip from the harbour. One of the best charter agencies in the area is **Aegean Yachting** ⓣ 0252 316 1517 ⓕ 0252 316 5749 ⓦ www.aegeanyacht.com

Day Gület Trip ★★★

There is a huge choice of boats offering day trips from the harbour. You will sail around several islands in the Gulf of Gökova, one of the prime sailing landscapes in the Mediterranean, and stop for swimming at lunchtime. Camel Bay is a popular stop. Most trips follow the same itinerary: out to Kara Ada Island with its hot springs, then on to Ada Boğazi for snorkelling. The final stop is at Kargı, with its camel rides.

RESTAURANTS (see map on page 39)

Ali Doksan €–€€ ❶ This typical *lokanta* is a down-to-earth place where you can examine the freshly cooked dishes and make your choice. It is the perfect place for a break from shopping, but get there before the local lunch crowd packs the tables at around 13.00 hours. Indoor and outdoor dining. ⓐ Inci Mah (across from the post office in the bazaar) ⓣ 0232 316 6687 ⓛ Open 11.00–14.00

Bodrum has a wide range of handicrafts and boutiques

Antique Theatre Hotel €€€ ❷ This is easily the best restaurant in town. The owners of the excellent small hotel have lived in Paris for many years and have brought haute cuisine to the Aegean. The tables spill out from a small dining room around the pool and the menu uses the finest ingredients (it includes champagne sauces). Antique Theatre has received excellent press reviews around the world. It is certainly a great place to book if you feel inclined to splash out. ⓐ Kibris Sehitler Caddesi 243 (across from the ancient theatre) ⓣ 0252 316 6053 ⓛ Open 19.00–22.00

Denizhan €€€ ❸ Opened in 1988, this is a great upmarket Turkish kitchen that has not lost sight of its roots. Known locally as '*Et-Lokantasi*' (meat restaurant), it is a carnivore's delight where even the humble kebab is turned into an event with metre-long skewers

brought to your table. The management recently opened the Denizhan Bistrot in downtown Bodrum (Neyzen Tevfik Caddesi), with a light menu of sandwiches, grills, pastas, and *carpaccios*. ⓐ Turgut Reis Yolu (about 2.5 km/1.5 miles west of town across from the Tofas/Fiat Garage) ⓣ 0252 363 7674 ⓦ www.denizhan.com ⓛ Open noon–midnight

Epsilon €€–€€€ ❹ Presided over by a Dutch flute player (who plays for guests when the mood takes her), Epsilon serves excellent Turkish/Greek-style cuisine, including some good, slow-cooked 'stew'-type dishes with the meat so tender that it falls apart. This is a place to relax in the heart of the old town. She also holds art exhibitions so you can shop and eat at the same time. ⓐ Turkkuyusa Mah, Keles Cikmazi 5 ⓣ 0252 313 2964 ⓛ Open 19.00–midnight, closed Nov–Apr

Kodacon €€€ ❺ Traditional Turkish and Mediterranean dishes are served in this more formal establishment. The garden, with its old olive press, makes a wonderful place to eat in the centre of town. Seafood combines with traditional Ottoman dishes. ⓐ Saraya Sokak 1, near the mosque in the inner harbour ⓣ 0252 316 3705 ⓛ Open 19.00–00.30; closed Nov–Apr ⓘ Reservations recommended

Secret Garden €€€ ❻ The English owner concentrates on excellent and varied Mediterranean cuisine, including authentic frogs' legs, *moules marinière* and *crème brulée*. There is a verdant garden setting for those sultry evenings. ⓐ Daneci Sokak 20, Eski Çeşme Mah ⓣ 0252 313 1641 ⓛ Open 19.30–midnight (Tues–Sun); closed Nov–Mar

Sünger Pizza € ❼ This is a long-standing and popular casual meeting place serving arguably the best pizza in town. The roof terrace offers great views over the harbour. ⓐ Neyzen Tevfik Caddesi 218 ⓣ 0252 316 0854 ⓛ Open 11.00–midnight

◀ *Club Bodrum floats out to sea every night (see page 46)*

Tarihi Yunuslar Karadeniz Pastanesi ❽ Traditional Turkish 'pudding' shop where you can stop for a post-dinner or pre-club sugar injection. A Bodrum institution. ⓐ Dr Alim Bey Caddesi ⓛ Open 08.00–midnight

NIGHTLIFE (see map on page 39)

Bar Street One long alleyway runs for a mile one block in from the water's edge. It is officially known by two names, Dr Alim Bey Caddesi (Street) and Cumhuriyet Caddesi (its more recently acquired name), but is known to everyone in Bodrum as 'Bar Street', where the music and the waiters vie for your money. Head for whatever sound you like, from top-40 pop to techno, but here are a few venues you may want to try.

Club Bodrum ❾ One of the most unusual nightclubs in Turkey, Club Bodrum is set on a catamaran that heads out to sea every night so you can 'boogie' offshore. There is a glass dance floor so you can enjoy the sea life while you cavort to music played by guest DJs. The boat returns to shore at 05.00 hours, but you can leave early by getting the club taxi back to shore. ⓐ Dr Alim Bey Caddesi 44 ⓣ 0252 313 3600 ⓦ www.clubbodrum.com ⓛ Open 01.00–05.00

Hadigari ❿ Turkish for 'let's go', Hadigari is a combined restaurant, bar and nightclub. Jazz music accompanies dinner, but later the music changes to dance and trance. It has a hipper clientele than some of the bars along 'Bar Street'. ⓐ Dr Alim Bey Caddesi 37 ⓣ 0252 313 1960 ⓛ Open 18.00–04.00, dinner 18.00–midnight

Halikarnas ⓫ The Bodrum legend, Halikarnas, is one of the most famous clubs in the world. With a capacity of 5000, it is a huge place and employs all the toys and ploys to make your night as memorable as possible, including the odd celebrity client. If you come to Bodrum, you really cannot go home without coming here. ⓐ Cumhuriyet Caddesi 178 ⓣ 0252 316 8000 ⓛ Open 22.00–05.00

Küba Bar ⓬ A favourite among wealthy Turks, this courtyard bar/ restaurant plays jazz and Latin music and has a much more low-key atmosphere than some of the other bars in the street. The restaurant is expensive. ⓐ Neyzen Tevfik Caddesi 62 ⓣ 0252 313 4450 ⓛ Open 21.00–04.00

M&M ⓭ Another excellent club that is a favourite – you will need to dress up to get in here. Great music with regular guest DJs from around Europe. ⓐ Dr Alim Bey Caddesi 4 ⓣ 0252 316 2725 ⓛ Open 22.00–05.00

Mavi ⓮ Bodrum's oldest café still attracts Turkish intellectuals through the day who come here to read their papers while enjoying a morning coffee or afternoon *rakı*. As the sun sets it is a great place to enjoy live Turkish music and has a much more authentic feel than some of the disco bars along the street. ⓐ Cumhuriyet Caddesi 175 ⓣ 0252 316 3932 ⓛ Open 07.00–02.00

Red Lion ⓯ There is always a lively atmosphere here – one of the longest established club/bars in town. You can come dressed to impress, and will be able to get your favourite cocktails and enjoy great music every night. ⓐ Cumhuriyet Caddesi 137 ⓣ 0252 316 3748 ⓦ www.redlion.com.tr ⓛ Open 11.00–03.00

Mumlu ⓰ This converted Ottoman mansion offers a great Turkish night out with dinner and folkloric performances. ⓐ Taslik Sokak, Taslik Cikmazi ⓣ 0252 313 8462 ⓛ Open 20.30–00.30. Performances from 21.00 hours

Sensi Bar ⓱ Sensi has a little bit of everything and is a popular choice with holidaying Brits. English and Scottish football games, karaoke and almost evening long 'happy hours' are the major draws. ⓐ Cumhuriyet Caddesi 149 ⓣ 0252 316 6845 ⓦ www.sensibar.com ⓛ Open 11.00–04.00

PARK PALAS

Gümbet
days of sun and nights of fun

Gümbet has really come of age over the last decade. It started life as a satellite of nearby Bodrum, providing hotel accommodation for the more established resort. Today it is a fully fledged destination in its own right, with a loyal band of mainly young fans.

Gümbet (pronounced Guumbet) does not have any highbrow intentions. There are no ancient sites or museums to put on your itinerary. What it does provide is everything you need for a fun-filled foreign holiday.

The beach has lots of fine sand, and a gentle gradient with shallow water make it perfect for sun worshippers, families and water-sports enthusiasts. The streets are crammed with restaurants and bars serving English, Chinese, Mexican and even Japanese food – plus Turkish, of course – and in the evenings when the strings of rope lights come on at dusk, the resort starts buzzing with music from the hundreds of bars whose tables line the streets. You can party till dawn here – it is not a place that will suit those who are looking for peace and quiet.

Gümbet means 'water cistern', a reference to the white, round-domed water-collection buildings that dot the Bodrum peninsula.

THINGS TO SEE & DO

Because Gümbet is only a couple of kilometres from Bodrum, you will be able to enjoy all 'Things to see & do' (see page 38) of Bodrum as well as the following:

Boat trips ★★★

There is a huge choice of boat trips. You will sail around several islands in the Gulf of Gökova with a stop for swimming and, of course, for lunch. **Camel Bay** is a popular stop. Here you can enjoy a ride on one of these rather unpredictable 'ships of the desert'. Most trips follow the same

The fine sand at Gümbet

itinerary, heading out to **Kara Ada Island** with its hot springs, then moving on to **Ada Boğazi** for snorkelling. The final stop is at **Kargı**, which also has camel rides.

Cinema ★

The Oasis shopping mall (see box, below) has a five-screen complex featuring Hollywood blockbusters in English with Turkish subtitles.

Water sports ★★★

Kiosks on the beach offer a full range of activities, from jet skiing and parasailing to banana boat rides. You can rent by the hour or by the session.

RESTAURANTS

Angus Steak House €€ The views across Gümbet Bay from the terrace are a lovely accompaniment to your meal. The restaurant serves a range of Turkish dishes, but it is the steaks (not surprising given the name) that have gained a reputation since they opened in 1993. ⓐ Sakir Esendemir Sokak 4 ⓣ 0252 313 3992 ⓛ Open 18.00–01.00

The Green Dragon €€ Opened in 1990, this was the first Chinese restaurant in the resort. It has branched out into other types of food and you can now enjoy Indian, Mexican, Italian and Turkish here – there should be something for everyone. ⓐ Gümbet Mevkii, Ayaz Caddesi ⓣ 0252 316 1504 ⓛ Open 11.00–midnight

SHOPPING

Aside from the normal souvenir shops, Gümbet has the Bodrum peninsula's first shopping mall – **Oasis** – with well-known names such as Quicksilver, Cacharel and Marks & Spencer. ⓐ Kibris Sehitleri Caddesi ⓣ 0252 317 0002 ⓦ www.oasisbodrum.com

Hong Kong Restaurant €€ Full choice of delicious Chinese dishes – Hong Kong concentrates on one type of cuisine and does it well. There is a small oriental-style veranda where you can eat outdoors. ⓐ Turgutreis Caddesi 406/A ⓣ 0252 313 4800 ⓒ Open 11.00–midnight

Windy Bay Beach Steak and Wine House € A cheap and cheerful place for a quick lunch. It is on Bar Street, which means it is a great pit-stop when you get the munchies during the evening. Concentrates on burgers, pizzas and omelettes – plus an English Sunday lunch. ⓐ Ayaz Caddesi ⓒ Open 08.00–01.00

Yucca €€€ One of the trendiest spots in Gümbet, catering for almost all types of food. Live entertainment is available after 22.00 hours daily and the place is always busy, so be sure to go early. ⓐ Adnan Menderes Caddesi 55 ⓒ Open 11.00–01.00

NIGHTLIFE

Mystery Bar The Mystery Bar is one of the late-evening haunts; below is the karaoke bar, which is always good for a laugh. Either dance or sit on bar stools in this stylish disco with futuristic metallic decor, including blue walls and silver tables. ⓐ Bar Street (Ayaz Caddesi) ⓣ 0252 313 1868 ⓒ Open 11.00–04.00

Outback Bar This famous Aussie surf bar has become an institution with its great beach location, signature fishbowl cocktails, good old rock music, pool and relaxed attitudes. Outback Bar 2 is now open, so you have two places from which to watch the sunset and sun rise. ⓦ www.theoutbackbar.com ⓒ Open 24 hours

Talk of the Town Three UK drag artists star in the nightly Dreamgirls show. They dress lavishly and pepper their acts with plenty of saucy British humour. ⓘ Admission includes dinner and a drink ⓐ Adnan Menderes Caddesi 20 ⓣ 0252 313 4621 ⓒ Open 19.30–02.00

The Bodrum Peninsula
for 'getting away from it all'

The verdant rocky coastline of the Bodrum peninsula is one of the world's top yachting destinations, with numerous attractive anchorages where a private dinner can be enjoyed plus excellent swimming and snorkelling. The countryside is made up of a series of dramatic forested ridges now dotted with *gümbets* (traditional water cisterns), stone towers, ruined churches and windmills.

Scattered around are a handful of small and exclusive resorts where you can take it easy and simply enjoy that novel you always meant to read, or snorkel in the pristine waters. These resorts are really all about quiet relaxation – although you will find excellent restaurants, nightlife is limited to an after-dinner stroll along the beach or a cocktail under the stars. However, all these resorts offer easy bus or taxi access to Bodrum and Gümbet for days of sightseeing and nights of action for those who want it.

Bitez ★★

Bitez is the biggest of these peninsula resorts, and the second most popular resort in Turkey for windsurfers after Çesme (see page 12). It is also an important marina, although the beach is small.
ⓐ 10 km (6 miles) from Bodrum

Dedeman Resort This has the Life Style Health and Beauty Centre, covering an area of 2250 sq m (2462 sq yd), with sauna, massage, solarium, Turkish bath and Jacuzzi plus fitness classes. There is also a 'Freshtaurant' with healthy food and drinks. ⓐ Gündönümü Mevkii, Bitez ⓣ 0252 313 8500 ⓦ www.dedemanhotels.com

◀ *Bitez resort is a sunbather's paradise*

Spafuga This small but well-equipped spa in a 'boutique' hotel offers shiatsu, aromatherapy and other massage treatments. ⓐ Fuga Hotel, Asarlık Mevkii ⓣ 0252 317 2360 ⓦ www.fuga.com.tr

Gümüşlük ★★★

The prettiest of the peninsula's settlements, Gümüşlük is subject to a preservation order and its centre is traffic free. The name is taken from a form of silver, which used to be mined close by, although locals say that it is because the sea is phosphorescent and glows in the dark at certain times of the year. The modern sleepy village occupies the site of ancient Myndos and you can wander among what is left of the ruins. ⓐ 23 km (14 miles) from Bodrum

Ortakent ★★

This inland village offers access to a number of beaches, including the 2 km (1.2 mile) long Yahşi Yalı and Kargi or Camel Beach – reached also on many day boat trips from Bodrum – where you can take a camel ride. The town has one of the finest examples of the traditional stone towers, the 17th-century Mustafa Paşa Tower. ⓐ 12 km (7 miles) from Bodrum

Torba ★

The modern resort of Torba makes a great base for water sports and sailing, but there are also ancient remains to explore – a round stone structure said to be 2500 years old plus a Byzantine monastery left to the elements long ago. ⓐ 8 km (5 miles) north of Bodrum

Turgutreis ★

Turgutreis is named after a famous Turkish naval commander, Derya Turgut Reis, who lived there in the 16th century. Today Turgutreis is a magnet for sailors, with a large marina, but it also has some amazing renovated Ottoman mansions clinging to the forested hillsides rising from the waterline. ⓐ On the south-west tip of the peninsula, 5 km (3 miles) from the Greek Island of Kos (see page 90)

The large marina at Turgutreis

Göltürkbükü ★★

This upmarket little enclave (pronounced Gerl-tuurk-buu-kuu), made up of Türkbükü and its neighbouring village Gölköy, is the summer home of many arty types from Istanbul. Those who do not have houses here arrive on their yachts. There is no beach here and swimming is from a concrete lido. ⓐ On the northern coast of peninsula, north of Bodrum

RESTAURANTS

Ali Rıza'nın Yeri €€ On the waterfront at Gümüşlük, this fish restaurant is one of the best, with a long-standing local clientele. It is not very expensive for fish (although of course fish is always the most expensive dish), and the quality is good. ⓐ Yalı Mevkii, Gümüşlük ⓣ 0252 394 3047

Daphne Restaurant €€€ There is a beautiful verdant garden for summer dining at this new, modern-designed restaurant, which takes the best local ingredients to produce international dishes. There is also a selection of fresh seafood. ⓐ Gözütok Sokak 4, Bitez ⓣ 0252 363 7722 ⓛ Open 10.30–midnight; holds a brunch on weekends at 11.00–15.00 hours, and there is live music at 21.00–23.00 hours

Gumuşcafé €–€€ With its pretty waterside setting, this small café makes a good place for a relaxed meal. The menu is quite extensive, with some excellent Turkish casseroles as well as French and Italian dishes. Vegetarians and vegans are also catered for. Snacks are served throughout the day. ⓐ Yalı Mevkii, Gümüşlük ⓣ 0252 349 4234 ⓛ Open 08.00–02.00

Mado € Part of a chain of Turkish 'patisseries', Mado serves excellent ice cream plus snacks such as *borek* and toasted sandwiches. Perfect for a light lunch. ⓐ Sah Caddesi, Bitez Yolu Mevkii 16, Bitez ⓣ 0252 363 9231 ⓛ Open 09.00–01.00

Mehtap Restaurant €€ Open for 20 years, this fish restaurant was one of the first in the resort. It overlooks a small marina and offers a good selection of fresh fish and grilled meats. ⓐ Akyarlar, Turgutreis ⓣ 0252 393 6148 ⓛ Open noon–midnight

Sakız Ana € An excellent family kitchen restaurant where you can try authentic, fresh, home-cooked Turkish cuisine. No frills, just tasty food, at lunchtimes only. ⓐ Yahşi 133, Ortakent ⓣ 0252 348 3703 ⓛ Open noon–17.00

Palavra Balık Restaurant €€ Set on the beach, the dining room and kitchens of this family-run restaurant are in a 200-year-old building. The vegetables and salad come direct from the garden and the fish straight from the sea. Prices are surprisingly low. ⓐ Ortakent Yahşi Beldesi ⓣ 0252 358 6290 ⓛ Open 08.00–midnight

EXCURSIONS
Out & about

Around the Aegean

THINGS TO SEE & DO

A Turkish evening ★★★

Genuine Turkish food and entertainment may be difficult to find in many modern resorts, but the 'Turkish evening' offers the perfect introduction to the culture and it is a really fun evening out. You will start with a buffet meal of *meze* dishes, barbecued meats and salads washed down with local wine or beer (see page 94 for more details of traditional foods), after which you will be entertained by folkloric dances, plus of course the famous 'belly dance'. Someone from the audience is always invited to have a go, which is generally amusing for everyone watching. Later in the evening the dance floor is handed over to the guests for an hour or so of disco dancing.

Gület cruise ★★★

It is really not a true Turkish holiday if you do not get out onto the water. From offshore you can really appreciate the beauty of the landscape, the verdant pine forests, olive groves and unspoilt beaches and coves. You may even be lucky enough to spot a dolphin or a turtle.

The *gület*, a traditional Turkish wooden boat, is one of the most beautiful and distinctive crafts in the Mediterranean and you will find them in all Turkish ports. You can rent them privately, but there is a choice of day trips for a very reasonable price. You can enjoy lunch and take a swim before returning back to your resort at about 17.00 or 18.00 in time to shower and change for your evening meal.

Jeep or 4x4 safari ★★★

The jeep safari is a real adventure. Out and about on roads you would probably never find yourself in a rental car, it gives you a chance to see

the traditional Turkish way of life and discover the countryside around your resort. The day includes a traditional lunch and a spot of shopping at a craft market or carpet warehouse. Routes vary with each company, but the following are some of the places you might head out to from the main resorts:

From Çeşme The rocky and sparsely populated Çeşme peninsula is the perfect place to get 'off the beaten track'. Head out to marvel at the old and often abandoned Greek villages, not populated since the 1920s.

From Kuşadası You can drive south to the Dilek National Park on the Davutlar peninsula, one of the last refuges of the rare Anatolian wild cat. After visiting the fortifications and driving through some spectacular forest scenery you can take a dip in the fresh spring water in the Zeus cave.

From Bodrum Explore the interior of the Bodrum peninsula and its numerous small villages – including Ciftikkoy, Etrim or Mumcular – plus some breathtaking forest and mountain scenery. You stop at a remote cove for a swim before returning to your hotel.

Village tours ★★

Most Aegean resorts have lost their traditional ways of life, so a village tour is the perfect way to see how the vast majority of Turks live. Visit a rural Turkish home where the women cook and make tea, enter a local mosque or watch carpet weaving and other traditional crafts.

From Kuşadası Visit Şirince, an old Greek hill town which is known for its traditional 19th-century village houses, handicrafts and rural way of life. Wine is produced in this small hillside Turkish village.

From Bodrum Take a trip through fragrant pine forest to the farming village of Çamlik.

From Çeşme Go to the peninsula villages, where decaying Greek mansions and windmills are set among the orange groves.

Shop in the markets ★

Inland towns hold large regional markets, usually once a week, and they are a great place to shop somewhere different from the tourist bazaars in the main resorts. Turks travel from small villages all around the area to shop for food and livestock and to socialize. It is a great place to watch them bargaining over prices or enjoying a tea in the cafés.

A sizeable town inland from Bodrum and its satellite resorts, Milas holds one of the largest and most authentic markets in the area. Fake designer labels sit side by side with a huge range of Turkish handicrafts, but the market is particularly known for its good selection of carpets. The traditional colours of Milas carpets are more muted than those of carpets produced in other areas, but there is a good choice from around Turkey. Because it is not just a tourist market, prices are generally less expensive than those in the resorts.

From Kuşadası and Altınkum, Söke is the place to be – the Wednesday market is not quite as large as the one at Milas, but the range of goods on offer is good and again you can enjoy the authentic atmosphere.

A wide range of Turkish handicrafts at a typical Turkish market

Turkish Baths ★★★

Not only will you be squeaky clean and relaxed, but your suntan will last far longer. So what better reason to try a traditional Turkish bath, or as the Turks call it, a *hammam*.

History Cleanliness is very important in Islamic cultures, where face, hands and feet must be clean before each prayer session. The communal *hammams* were a place where hot water could be guaranteed and where men or women could come and have a good gossip. During Ottoman times it was grounds for divorce if a man refused his wife bath money. Today, although many town houses and apartments have all the mod cons, it is still a popular social activity.

What to expect Traditional *hammams* have separate sessions for men and women, but the owners of *hammams* in tourist areas understand that visitors have different attitudes and will run mixed sessions.

When you enter a *hammam* you are given a *peştama* (gown) and wooden sandals to wear. You can go naked under the robe or wear a swimming costume, bikini or shorts.

Then you go into the *hararet*, or steam room, where you are hit by a wall of hot air. Go to one of the basins and wash yourself all over. When you wash the suds off, do not get any back in the basin because this needs to be kept clean for other customers. You then lie on the *göbek taşi*, or naval stone, the marble slab at the centre of the room. Relax for 15 minutes or so to let the heat open up the pores. Your masseur or *tellak* will then rub you with a rough cloth covered in soap to slough off any grime and dead skin cells. Then you are pummelled and rubbed until you feel as though your arms and legs might fall off. After another shower, you leave the hot room, wrap yourself in a thick robe and relax with a cup of tea. Do not rush this part because you need to cool down and let your body adjust to the treatment.

Foça

The perfect place for an afternoon of relaxed sightseeing, Foça is a fishing village turned resort that has not yet lost its charm. It is a favourite spot for weekenders from nearby Izmir, so you will be among Turks relaxing and enjoying themselves. They come to stroll in the old town, sit in the cafés and eat at the excellent authentic restaurants along the seafront.

Foça tourist office ⓐ Sahil Caddesi, in the main square ⓣ 0232 812 1222

HISTORY

Founded by Ionian peoples in around 1000 BC, the town was originally Phocaea. The city became known for its shipbuilding and seafaring skills. Its huge ships, powered by 50 or more oarsmen, sailed all around the Mediterranean. It is even said that the Phocaeans landed in southern France and founded a settlement that is now the city of Marseilles. Later, Phocaea became a Byzantine trading port before being given as a gift to the Genoese who protected the trade routes to western Europe. It finally fell into the hands of the Ottomans when it settled down as a simple fishing village.

THINGS TO SEE & DO

Ancient theatre ★

This small theatre dates from *c.* 340 BC. ⓐ On the eastern outskirts of town.

Beşkapılar (the Castle) ★★

This part Byzantine/part Genoese structure dominates the waterfront and is the most impressive building in town, although it has been rather crudely renovated and had a couple of towers added. ◷ It is not open to the public

Boat trips ★★

In ancient Greek, *phocaea* means 'seal' and the town took its name from the noisy monk seals that populated the bay's rocky shores and islets. Today, the few that are left are protected by the Turkish government, but you can take a trip from the harbour to watch them lazing on the rocks.

Fatih Camii ★

Built in the 15th century after the Ottoman takeover, this small mosque has some delicate interior decoration. ⓐ Eski Adliye Sokak

Old Town ★★

A tiny maze of alleyways makes up the old town and you can wander among whitewashed cottages and Ottoman mansions that now house boutiques and café/bars.

Old town of Foça

Pergamum

One of the most dramatic ancient sites in Turkey, Pergamum was capital of the region of Asia Minor in the 3rd century BC before Ephesus took over (see page 73). The city was the 'Harley Street' of its day, with an important medical school, and people travelled to it from all corners of the empire for treatment.

Historical records tell us that Pergamum had beautiful and ornate buildings, but when the first archaeologists arrived from Germany in the 19th century, they took the best bits home with them and many of them are now on display at the Pergamum Museum in Berlin. However, the city is not a disappointment – the stunning location and marvellous theatre make it worth a visit, as is the nearby modern town of Bergama, famed for its carpets.

Ruins of Pergamum

HISTORY

Founded in 301 BC, the city was Rome's first friendly ally in the area, but although it grew rich and powerful very quickly, by the 2nd century AD it had lost its influence. The two main archaeological sites, the Acropolis (upper city) and the Asclepion (ancient centre of healing), lie a few kilometres apart. Much of ancient Pergamum probably lies undiscovered underneath the family homes you see today.

HIGHLIGHTS

Acropolis ★★

Located 280 m (919 ft) up above the surrounding countryside, the Acropolis has a spectacular setting, with panoramic city views out towards the Aegean. The theatre, with as many as 78 rows of seats, cascades down the steep natural drop of the hill. On the hilltop plateau sit the partly re-erected remains of the 2nd century AD Temple of Trajan. ⓐ Kale Yolu, signposted 5 km (3 miles) above the town ⓑ Open 08.00–19.00 (May-Oct); 08.00–17.00 (Nov–Apr) ⓘ Admission charge

Asclepion ★

This ancient health complex was state of the art during the Roman era, 2000 years ago. You can walk along the western section of Via Tecta, a marble colonnaded road that connected the Acropolis to the sanctuary, and explore the remains of a temple complex and diagnosis room. ⓐ Asclepion Caddesi, signposted a kilometre south of the town, off the main road ◷ Open 08.00–19.00 (May–Oct); 08.00–17.00 (Nov–Apr) ⓘ Admission charge

Archaeological Museum ★

Although many of Pergamum's finest treasures are now overseas, there are still a few at the site. The figure of Nike (Winged Victory) displayed here has become an emblem of the city and there are elements of ornate friezes and pediments that hint at the splendour now missing. One of the most impressive pieces, a statue of Aphrodite, was found at another site nearby. The museum also has a small selection of later traditional costumes and handicrafts in its ethnography section. ⓐ Bankalar Caddesi ◷ Open 08.30–17.30 (Tues–Sun), closed Mon ⓘ Admission charge

Red Basilica ★

Originally built as a Temple to the Egyptian Gods Harpokrates, Isis and Serapis in the 2nd century AD, this huge striking red stone building was converted into a Christian basilica in the 4th century (one of the original Seven Churches of Asia Minor) and now also has a mosque within the walls. ⓐ Intersection of Kasapoğlu Caddesi and Bankalar Caddesi ◷ Open 08.30–17.30 ⓘ Admission charge

EXCURSION

Bergama ★

The centre of Bergama has some excellent timber framed Ottoman mansions in its old quarter, where you can stroll amongst some of the Aegan's best carpet shops, selling traditional Bergama styles (characterized by their deep red colour) and some good antiques shops. Prices can be high here, but so is quality. ⓐ A few kilometres outside Pergamum

Sardis

Once an important ancient city, much of Sardis is hidden under the village of Sart and the farmland around it. There is not a lot to see – it is nowhere near the size of Pergamum or Ephesus – but each building or sector excavated is either of exceptional quality or beauty, or offers the visitor something unusual or interesting.

HISTORY

The discovery of gold in the River Pactolus close by guaranteed that Sardis would be a successful city. Founded 5000 years ago, it was capital of the Lydian Kingdom (*c.* 685 BC) and one of its rulers, King Croesus (*c.* 561–548 BC), was said to be the richest man in the world, giving rise to the saying 'rich as Croesus'. The Lydians were conquered by Alexander the Great but the city continued to thrive under Greek and Roman rule.

Ruins of Sardis

Temple of Artemis

HIGHLIGHTS

Imperial Hall ★★★

This 3rd-century AD two-storey brick and marble building was the town's bath and sports complex, but the front facade is one of the finest in Turkey, decorated with fluted columns, marble friezes and an intricately carved pediment crowning the two sets of entrance arches. Unfortunately, the 3 acre (1.2 ha) complex behind it is still mostly piles of stone and brick. The best time to view the facade is in the mornings, when the sun shines directly on it.

Marble Way ★★★

This is an excellent section of ancient roadway that has been carefully excavated in the heart of Sardis. The Byzantine boulevard is 18 m (20 ft) wide, with a thick marble base now worn by the cart tracks that passed along here for centuries. The road was lined with small shops, but now only the foundations of the walls and a few sections of mosaic can be seen.

Synagogue ★

The 3rd-century synagogue has some impressive decoration, particularly its mosaics. Those on the floor are original, but the wall decoration is reconstructed. The originals are in the museum in nearby Manisa.

ⓐ Main road in Sart ⓑ Open 08.30–20.00 (summer); 08.30–17.30 (winter) ⓘ Admission charge

Temple of Artemis ★

When archaeologists first arrived at the temple site in 1910, only the tops of two columns stuck out of the soil. Built *c.* 200 BC, the site had been abandoned after an earthquake in AD 17. Measuring 99 m by 45 m (108 by 49 yds), the temple was one of the largest religious sites in the Greek world, even larger than the Parthenon in Athens. The temple platform and a handful of Ionic columns convey an impression of the size and beauty of the finished temple. ⓐ A kilometre south of Sart, signposted from the village ⓑ Open 08.30–20.00 (summer); 08.30–17.30 (winter) ⓘ Admission charge

MYTHS OF THE RIVER PACTALUS

The Midas Touch

According to Greek myth, King Midas was responsible for putting the gold in the River Pactalus. The gods granted him his wish that everything he touched should turn to gold but when this became a curse – he could not eat or drink anything – he pleaded with the gods to take the power back. When he washed his hands in the river, the gold in his body was released into the water and Midas was mortal again.

The Golden Fleece

It is possible that there is a practical basis to the mythological story of the 'golden fleece'. In ancient times the Greeks would 'pan' for gold by putting sheepskins in the River Pactalus. Tiny pieces of metal on the river bottom would get caught in the fine wool. When the skin was taken out of the water and dried the gold would fall out and could be collected and smelted.

Izmir

The third largest city in Turkey and its largest port, Izmir does not make a good first impression. It is huge, hot and dusty, with hillsides festooned with concrete apartment blocks. But Izmir was once the ancient Greek city of Smyrna, and for many centuries the eastern terminus of the silk route from China, so it has a great history, plus one of the most authentic bazaars in western Turkey.

Traditional fishing in Izmir

HISTORY

Until World War I, the population of Izmir was mostly of Greek descent. These people had lived there since ancient times and stayed after the Ottomans took Turkey in the 15th century. Izmir saw some of the fiercest fighting during Turkey's War of Independence in the early 1920s, and much of the historic town was destroyed. Finally, the Greek population left en masse.

THINGS TO SEE & DO

Alsancak District ★★

Although large sections of the city burned to the ground in the violence of the 1920s, this small quarter escaped and displays some lovely 18th- and 19th-century Greek-style mansions. In the last 20 years, plenty of money has been poured into renovating the district, but you will also find characterful houses that are still in need of care and attention.

Archaeological Museum ★★★

This is one of the most comprehensive collections in Turkey, with pieces from all the major archaeological sites in the northern Aegean and all eras of the country's long history.

It is in these galleries that the daily lives of the people are brought to life with kitchen tools, decorative figurines, and intricate precious jewellery showing just how sophisticated these ancient peoples were. Larger statues and busts from the Hellenistic and Roman periods are equally impressive and have their own gallery, so you can explore how styles changed over time. ⓐ Bahri Baba Park ⓑ Open 08.30–17.30 (Tues–Sat), closed Mon ⓘ Admission charge

Ethnographic Museum ★★

Turkey has very few museums that showcase Turkish Ottoman history and traditional ways of life, but this is one of the best.

The building was constructed in neoclassical style and started life as St Roch Hospital in 1831. It was opened as the museum in 1984. All aspects of 19th-century life are covered here. One of the most

fascinating sections is the handicrafts exhibit, where you can see how many of the souvenirs you can buy today were made over 100 years ago. Other exhibits include clothing, glass, traditional costumes and the reconstruction of a bridal room plus books and coins. ⓐ Bahri Baba Park ◷ Open 08.30–noon and 13.00–17.00 (Tues–Sun) ❶ Admission charge

Roman Agora ★★

One of the biggest Roman *agoras* (marketplace and meeting area) in western Turkey, the remains here date from the 2nd century AD and include temples, shops and stoas. Excavations in the late 1990s unearthed the northern entrance gate and produced statues and smaller figurines plus lots of domestic items, including glass bottles and metal tools. ⓐ Anafartalar Caddesi ◷ Open 08.30–noon and 13.00–17.30 ❶ Admission charge

Bazaar ★★★

This is not a tourist city, so more than anywhere on the Aegean coast you can find a genuine eastern shopping experience here. The bazaar is divided into different quarters selling items as mundane as buckets and washing lines to gold and carpets. It is a great place to watch the locals striking a bargain over a cup of apple tea. ⓐ West of Anafartalar Caddesi

Atatürk Museum ★

The house itself is an interesting mixture of Greek and Ottoman styles and was owned by a Greek carpet merchant until he abandoned it in 1922. It was presented to Atatürk as a gift by the Municipality of Izmir in 1926. The president's private quarters were on the first floor and are still furnished in period style with a few of his personal belongings. ⓐ Atatürk Avenue No. 24, Alsancak ◷ Open 08.30–17.30 (Tues–Sun), closed Mon ❶ Admission charge

---

Izmir tourist office ⓐ Gazi Osman Paşa Bul in the Büyük Efes Hotel ⓣ 0232 484 4300

Ephesus

Ephesus is the largest and most complete ancient city in the eastern Mediterranean, situated 19 km (12 miles) north east of Kuşadası. It is a must-see site even if you are not into history. The exceptionally well-preserved buildings allow us to step back in time to life in the capital of late Roman Asia Minor with little touches that bring the citizens to life.

To see the architectural detail it is best to arrive early or late in the day when the site is quiet, but the crowded streets you find when the tour groups arrive (between 10.00 and 16.00 hours) offer the kind of genuine lively atmosphere that Ephesus would have had over 1500 years ago.

Ancient Roman city of Ephesus

HISTORY

Founded in the 11th century BC, Ephesus became an important and rich city because it was the centre of worship for Artemis, the goddess of fertility. The temple here was one of the seven wonders of the ancient world and attracted pilgrims from around ancient Greece.

In Roman times the city was capital of Asia Minor, with a population of over 250,000 people. It was a trading and banking city of immense wealth and was one of the most advanced cities in the empire, with both flushing communal latrines and street lighting.

Ephesus was an important Christian city in the middle of the first millennium, with a close association with St Paul of Tarsus, and was populated until the 11th century AD. The last few hundred years brought serious problems when its port on the River Cayster began to silt up. Eventually it was cut off from the sea completely, making trade impossible. The city was then abandoned.

Ephesus theatre

HIGHLIGHTS

Upper City ★

A plateau at the top of the hill is the least exciting part of the city. Around the wide space that was once the Upper Agora you will be able to explore the administrative headquarters of the city, a small *odeon* (theatre) and the remains of a thermal spa. The best part of the upper city is the view down over the rest of Ephesus. From the small square in front of the Monument of Memmius, which was erected in homage to the citizens of the city, you get your most breathtaking view down Curetes Street, one of the most photographed vistas in Turkey.

Beyond the buildings look out over the flat area where there is a modern airfield. This used to be the port area for the ancient city. Then search for the coast out in the distance. This is how far the sea has receded since Roman times and it shows why the city was doomed. There was no way to transport large amounts of goods efficiently over land in those days, and without a port, the city could not function.

Curetes Street ★★★

The major arterial route linking the upper city with the port, Curetes Street was the Oxford Street, Briggate or Princes Street of its day. Shops selling goods from around the empire lined the thoroughfare, along with a number of important temples in between, including the Temple of Hadrian (built *c.* AD 117–138), with its distinctive double archway of fine Corinthian columns and elaborate frieze dedicated to the goddess Tyche.

Slope House ★★★

On each side of Curetes Street, the residential quarters of Ephesus lie on the terraced hillside, reached by narrow alleyways. These were the houses of the rich, and one three-storey residence, Yamac Evleri, or 'Slope House', has undergone a thorough excavation to offer a glimpse of the Roman lifestyle and interior design. The spacious rooms are decorated with incredible original mosaic floors and wall frescoes that were the height of fashion. ❶ Entry to Slope House is extra to the Ephesus ticket price, but is well worth it

Celcus library

Celcus Library ★★★

At the bottom of Curetes Street, the library is one of the focal points of the city. Erected in AD 117 as a memorial to Tiberius Julius Celsus by his son, it has a grandiose two-storey facade decorated with fluted columns and statues depicting the Four Virtues: Goodness (Arete), Thought (Ennoia), Knowledge (Episteme) and Wisdom (Sophia). The library once held 12,000 scrolls and was considered a great centre of learning.

Gate of Mazeus & Mithridates ★★

Linking the Library and the neighbouring *agora*, the Gate of Mazeus and Mithridates was commissioned by two slaves freed by the Emperor Augustus who went on to become leading citizens of the city. It is built in the style of a triumphal arch.

Baths of Scolastica ★★

The baths were one of the social centres of the city, a place where men got together to do business deals, debate politics or simply gossip. These were built in the 1st century AD in the heart of the city almost opposite the Celcus Library, and you can see the hot room and cold room.

Theatre ★★

One of the prettiest and most complete Roman theatres, Ephesus theatre is still being used during the important Ephesus Festival of Culture and Art each May. During Roman times, 24,000 people would cram the stands to enjoy drama and comedy, and it was also the scene of many of St Paul's Evangelical speeches. He was cornered here by angry Ephesians when he criticized their beloved Artemis, but managed to escape.

Arcadian Way ★

One of the first Roman Streets to get municipal lighting, Arcadian Way led from the theatre to the port in the 5th century AD. The widest avenue in the city, much of it is now off limits to the public, but it is possible to stand at the top (in front of the theatre) and look towards what would have been the warehouse district and waterfront during Roman times.

Marble Way ★

Linking Curetes Street with Arcadian Way, the short Marble Way has a couple of interesting things to see. Notice how the marble of the road surface has been worn away by the passing of hundreds of thousands of cart wheels. No doubt these carts were heavily laden with goods for market. There is also an advertisement for a brothel etched in a stone of the road, pointing the way to the entrance close by.

Temple of Artemis ★

A kilometre away from the city is the Temple of Artemis or Artemision, the most important temple to Artemis in the world. A mammoth building measuring 105 by 55 m (96 by 60 yds) and housing a life-size gold statue to the goddess, it was so impressive that it was known as one of the seven wonders of the ancient world; today, it is a shadow of its former self. The Goths destroyed the site in AD 262 and much of the stone was later recycled, so that only the main temple platform and a couple of lonely columns remain.

Although the gold statue of Artemis has never been found (it was probably melted down centuries ago), there are several fascinating stone and marble statues of her in the Ephesus Museum at Selçuk (see page 88). ⓐ 500 m (547 yd) from Selçuk on the Kuşadası road
Open 08.30–17.30 Admission charge

Pamukkale

Pamukkale (Pamuk-kalay) means 'cotton castle' in Turkish and it is a very appropriate name. Inland from the Aegean coast, and more than a day trip, this huge natural travertine (a type of crystalline rock) fountain is one of Turkey's most famous attractions and one of its most beautiful and spectacular landscapes. Here, sparkling white terraces of shallow limestone pools rather like the shapes of oyster shells cling precariously to the hillside. From a distance they look like piles of raw cotton, a crop that you find in fields all across this part of the country. Close up, the limestone is brilliant white and its edges glitter like diamonds.

HIGHLIGHTS

The Travertine Cascades ★★★

This is the place where you will find the famed cascades, where several storeys of pure white shallow bowls, filled with azure blue waters, shimmer in the sunshine.

Unfortunately, Pamukkale's popularity has also brought problems. In the early days, there was no protection for this delicate environment. People broke the sides of the pools as they climbed over them and sun oils from swimmers left a residue in the water that discoloured the white limestone. To add to the situation, several hotels that had been built above the cascade were using water directly from the spring for

HOW IT HAPPENS

The hot springs that emerge from the top of the hill in Pamukkale are rich in minerals. As the water cascades down the side of the hill, it leaves a microscopic layer of these minerals in any undulation on the ground and in the bowls of the pools. This turns white as it hardens. Over millions of years, these thin layers have built up and in some places at Pamukkale they are metres thick.

their own private swimming pools – this meant that there was not enough spring water reaching the limestone pools to repair the damage.

By the early 1990s 'cotton castle' was in real danger of ruin. As a result, in the mid-1990s, the Turkish authorities instigated an action plan to save the cascades. The hotels on the plateau have now been bulldozed and the waters are being trained over the most damaged sections to make them white once again, a bit like the teeth-whitening process that is so fashionable at the moment. People have been banned from bathing in or walking on the pools. There is a footpath that you can follow as long as you take your shoes off, but it is a bit painful for soft feet. However, all these changes have made a tremendous difference in less than ten years and the total area of white limestone is beginning to expand again. ⓐ About 300 km (186 miles) north-east of Bodrum ● Open 24 hours a day, ticket office 08.00–19.00 (May–Oct); 08.00–17.00 (Nov–Apr) ● Admission charge when ticket office is open

Hierapolis ★★★

The Romans loved natural springs, which they thought could cure various ailments. Hierapolis, the city they built here on top of the plateau next to Pamukkale, was really a giant spa town. Walk down the Cardo, the colonnaded main street to the Gate of Dominitian or explore the necropolis (cemetery), with its collection of more than 1200 tombs and giant sarcophagi. The **museum** on site displays a range of items found during excavation of the site. ● Extra ticket charge

Pamukkale Thermal Baths ★★★

These baths have been open since Roman times and the modern buildings have been built directly on top of the ancient ones. In fact, while you are bathing, you can sit on fallen Roman columns that lie just under the surface of the water. The warm springs are said to be good for arthritis, stress and a long list of other ailments – although most people just come for the fun of swimming there. Even if you do not want to get wet (extra charge), come and have a look at the pools.

Aphrodisias

In ancient times, Aphrodisias was famous for its school of sculpture and art. Getting a place to study here virtually guaranteed a successful career. Because of the school, the city was one of the most beautifully decorated in the ancient world and the statues excavated here are some of the best at any ancient site in Europe.

HISTORY

Aphrodisias was founded in the 7th century BC as a centre of worship of Aphrodite, goddess of love and beauty, who gave the city its name. When a source of fine marble was discovered nearby, the school was founded and the city thrived from the 5th century BC. Unfortunately, the site was prone to earthquakes. This and the fall of the Roman Empire in the 4th century AD brought an end to the good times. People continued to live there but there was no money to repair the damaged buildings. The city was abandoned in the early 14th century to be replaced by a small rural village. Archaeologists did not get a chance to work on the site until 1956, when another earthquake forced the villagers to relocate.

The ticket office at Aphrodisias gives out a good map with a circular tour marked on it.

HIGHLIGHTS

Theatre ★

Hidden under a massive 40 m (131 ft) of earth until the 1970s, the theatre – semi-circular in design with white marble seating – was built into a natural hill. The *cavea* and stage were added when the Hellenistic design got a facelift during the Roman era, allowing gladiatorial contests.

South Agora ★

This huge market place was planned and built in the 1st century AD and originally had two porticos (covered walkways) of Ionic columns running 200 m (656 ft) down each flank. Some of these have been re-erected.

Excavations show that the Tiberius Portico at the southern flank was decorated with highly ornate friezes and inscriptions praising Emperor Tiberius. You can see examples of these in the museum (see below).

Temple of Aphrodite ★★

The centre of the city and its most important building, the temple was originally the centre of worship to the protector goddess of the city. Worshippers would have travelled from around Asia Minor to visit the site and this would have brought a lot of money to the area. It would have been a large and ornate structure, but only 14 of the 40 columns still remain. In the early Christian era (3rd–5th century AD) it was converted into a church and most of the ornate pagan decoration was destroyed. A large statue to the goddess was found just outside the temple precinct and this is on display in the museum.

Stadium ★★

The largest ancient stadium in Turkey and the best preserved in the whole Mediterranean, this is an impressive structure with a length of 262 m (287 yds) and a width of 60 m (65 yds) surrounded by well-preserved stands with a capacity of 30,000. The stadium was originally used for athletics competitions. It even held mini-Olympics-type competitions for the Asia Minor province. In the 7th century, after the theatre was damaged in an earthquake, it also held circus and wild-animal shows that were then the height of fashion.

Tetrapylon ★★★

The most beautiful of the remains discovered in the city, the tetrapylon is a monumental double archway built in the 2nd century AD at a major road junction in the city. Sixteen finely fluted Corinthian columns support a pediment of incredibly high craftsmanship.

Museum ★★★

This is one site where the European archaeologists did not get the chance to take all the best stuff to their own museums back home.

The collection here is stunning, probably the best museum of ancient sculpture in Turkey. Every work is of a high standard, but look particularly for the formal statue of the goddess Aphrodite carved with reliefs of the Three Graces, sun and moon god and cupid. All of these are symbols of the Aphrodite cult. Open 08.00–19.00 (May–Oct); 08.00–17.30 (Nov–Apr) Admission charge

Tetrapylon archway

The Menderes Valley & Bafa Gölü

a serenely scenic drive

This full-day tour links some of the Aegean's lesser-visited but equally prestigious ancient sites. Driving south from Kuşadası, this 200 km (120 mile) round trip takes in the Ionian settlement of Priene, the Roman remains of Miletus and the site of the famous Oracle at Didyma. The trip ends at the wonderfully serene Bafa Gölü (Lake Bafa) where you can enjoy a simple meal of fresh fish or *meze* (see page 94) before returning to your hotel. Better still, stay to watch the sunset over the water and enjoy the buzzing of the cicadas as night falls.

To start the tour, leave Kuşadası on the main road south (D515), and take a right turn just after the town of Söke signposted Priene (road number 09–55). The site is on the right just after the village of Güllübahçe.

HIGHLIGHTS

Priene ★★★

Set on a terraced hillside overlooking the Menderes Valley, the remains of Priene sit among magnificent mature fragrant pines in the lea of a rocky peak. Priene was originally founded on the valley bottom, but when its access to the sea silted up, the population moved up the hill to a new town in the 4th century BC, making Priene one of the world's first pre-planned settlements. The revolutionary layout of straight streets with intersections was designed by Hippodamus of Miletus in the 5th century BC. His theories spread through the known world and were used in the planning of modern cities like Paris and New York.

Temple of Athena The most important monument in the city is the Temple of Athena, built in the 3rd century BC with money given to the city by Alexander the Great, who stayed here in 334 BC.

Housing district The remains of hundreds of family homes can be seen on the far flank of the site (the western section), past the *agora* and *stoa*. Only the lower parts of the walls remain in place. There is a sign that indicated the very house where Alexander was invited to stay, probably by an important town official, but there is no evidence of this inside, and the structure does not look any different from the rest.

Stoa and Agora Sitting at a major intersection in the centre of Priene, the *stoa* and *agora* are built of monumental stone blocks with far less decoration than buildings found at Ephesus (see page 73) or Miletus (see below). The Romans had little influence here, especially in terms of the architectural style. The view from the remains of the *stoa* and the *agora* beyond is breathtaking. Open 08.30–18.30 (May–Oct); 08.30–17.30 (Nov–Apr) Admission charge

From Priene carry on along the main road – right at the junction. After about 8 km (5 miles) there is a turning left to Didyma (Didim). You will cross the River Menderes and see a signpost left to Miletus (Miletos).

Miletus (Miletos) ★

An important sea-port in ancient Greek times, Miletus was a large and very rich city. The principle port of entry to the region under the Greeks, Miletus was more important than Ephesus, but the Romans preferred Ephesus so influence shifted north. The other problem for Miletus was that it suffered even more than Ephesus from the silting up of its port. The site is now several kilometres from the sea and all this fertile farmland has been laid down in the last 1500–2000 years.

The theatre The largest in Turkey, this ancient theatre has not been renovated like the one at Ephesus. The *cavea* (seating area) and vaulted walkways underneath the cavea are well preserved, allowing you to

really explore the structure, including chambers where the wild animals would have been kept before gladiatorial contests. Above the theatre is a small Byzantine castle with views down over the whole structure.

The rest of the city The old harbour used to be behind the theatre. Two stone lions held the chain barring ships from entering when the harbour closed each winter. Along the marble-lined Sacred Way, which linked Miletus with Didyma, you can explore the remains of an agora, gymnasium and partially reconstructed Ionic stoa. Open 08.30–19.00 (May–Oct); 08.30–17.30 (Nov–Apr) Admission charge

From Miletus rejoin the main road and continue towards the modern village of Didyma (Didim), passing through the village of Akköy as you go.

Didyma (Didim) ★★

Perhaps the most impressive single monument on the west coast, this temple was the third largest structure of the ancient Greek world when it was built. It was surrounded by 124 marble columns and decorated with some of the best sculptures and friezes in the empire.

This is the site where the Greek god Zeus came down to earth to make love to the goddess Leto, who then gave birth to twins Artemis and Apollo. Over time, the sacred spring at the site became famous throughout the ancient Greek world as the site of a powerful oracle, dedicated to Apollo.

In 494 BC the oracle was destroyed by the Persians and the spring dried up, but it began to flow again when Alexander the Great called in for a consultation in 334 BC. The Oracle proclaimed Alexander 'Son of Zeus', which boosted his image and put the Oracle back at the top of its game.

By the 3rd century AD, Christianity had become well established in the area and the sanctuary fell gradually into disuse. In AD 385, it was officially closed on the orders of the Byzantine Emperor Theodosius.

The porch The entrance to this temple consists of a monumental staircase and an entrance porch that is one of the most complete and impressive in Turkey. Over 100 of the columns are still standing (although only three of these are to their full height) and still form a curtain around the inner chamber.

Inner Chamber Reached by two narrow, sloping tunnels, the inner sanctum was where the power of the Oracle was contained. Off limits to everyone but the priests and priestesses, it was divided into living quarters, sacred sanctums and consulting rooms. Now it is a single large and semi-open space.

The 'Furious Medusa' An exquisite marble head adorns the steps at the entrance to the site. An emblem of the southern Aegean, its image can be found on postcards and tourist brochures. Although christened the 'furious Medusa' by local Turks, archaeologists now think that this is the god Apollo, patron of the temple. Open 08.00–19.00 (May–Oct); 08.00–17.00 (Nov–Apr) Admission charge

From Didyma retrace your steps back to Akköy and then turn right, travelling through the countryside until you reach the main Kuşadası/

THE ROLE OF THE ORACLE

In the ancient world, the gods and goddesses decided the fate of all mortals. The Oracle was said to be able to speak to these gods, and rich and influential people came to the Oracle for consultations hoping that the gods would look favourably on them.

Of course, mortals could not talk directly to the Oracle or to the gods. That was the job of the priests or priestesses who served here. They had the secret of how to get the answers, perhaps by spells, incantations and natural hallucinogenic gases.

Bodrum road. Turn right and follow the road until you reach the village of Bafa. Turn left here, signposted Kapıkırı, following the twisting road to the lakeshore 14 km (9 miles) away.

The 'Furious Medusa'

Bafa Gölü (Lake Bafa) ★★

Bafa Gölü, also known as 'Lake Bafa', is a slightly salt-water lake that was formed when the mouth of Latmos Gulf was cut off from the sea. Today it covers over 100 sq km (62 miles) and is surrounded by the barren, treeless peaks of the Latmos Mountain range. Tantalizing remains of Roman buildings and later Byzantine towers and churches sit on the water's edge and on small islands offshore. You can visit these on a boat trip.

Around the lake In the hills behind the lake's edge are more remains of the city of **Heracleia ad Latmos**, some of which lie side by side with the modern farming community of **Kapıkırı** (❶ there is a ticket office for the site just before the village centre; you need to buy a ticket during the day). The village itself provides a fascinating insight into rural Turkey, with donkeys still used as transport and crops tended by hand. The women will want to sell you their handmade lace, which is a thriving cottage industry here.

Turn down to the lake's edge (left just before the site ticket office) and you will reach a couple of small family-owned restaurants including **Zeybeks** (☎ 0252 543 5158). This is the place to relax after your drive and take in the magnificent view.

Selçuk

The little town of Selçuk is the closest community to Ephesus, so it has been rather thrust into the spotlight in recent years. The excellent Ephesus Museum is the most important reason to visit, but the town has other historical attractions that would fill an extra couple of hours.

THINGS TO SEE & DO

Ephesus Museum ★★★

If you visit the site of Ephesus (see page 73) then you must also visit Ephesus Museum. This is where the best of the artefacts found at the site are on display. The museum is not too big and overwhelming. The first gallery, a recreation of a Roman room excavated at the site, is complete with furniture and a small domestic shrine. The range of everyday objects on display is impressive, from hair pins to leather sandals. More precious objects include gold filigree jewellery and fine Samian tableware. Several rooms display monumental statuary and friezes that decorated temples and public buildings.

Room 7 is set aside for statues of the goddess Artemis, the patroness of Ephesus and goddess of fertility, but the final room is the Hall of the Emperors, where statues and busts of many Roman leaders have been brought together. ⓐ Agora Çarşısı ⓑ Open 08.00–noon; 13.30–17.30 (Tues–Sun); closed Mon ⓘ Admission charge

Basilica of St John ★

If this 5th-century AD church were still complete it would be the seventh largest cathedral in the world. Built to honour the burial site of the apostle St John the Evangelist, who settled here in the 1st century AD, the church was erected using the finest marbles and semi-precious stones. The remains of the nave wall give the best impression of how large and impressive the church would have been. If you find this hard to imagine,

Remains of the Basilica of St John

look at the drawing on the information panel on the site, which depicts the complete structure.

An impressive 6th-century AD castle, **Ayasoluk** stands over the site with demanding views across the valley. ⓐ St John Caddesi ⓑ Open 08.00–17.00 ⓘ Admission fee

Işa Bey Mosque ★

Built in the 14th century, this is one of the oldest working mosques in the region and is worth a visit for its architectural beauty. It was built by the Seljuk's, who ruled this land before the arrival of the Ottomans, but the interior is decorated in both Seljuk and Ottoman style, making it an important transitional building. Once inside, look at the column capitals that support the domes – one is a recycled Roman column, most probably taken from Ephesus. ⓐ St John Caddesi ⓑ Open all hours except during prayers ⓘ Admission free

EXCURSIONS

Meryemana ★

This is one of the most important religious sites in Turkey, and a place revered by both Christians and Muslims. Discovered in 1891, this shady spot beside a babbling brook is said to be the home and final resting place of the Virgin Mary. Known in Turkish as *Meryemana* (House of the Virgin Mary), the site was visited by Pope Paul VI in 1967, when he approved the site as genuine.

A simple Byzantine chapel now sits on the spot where the Madonna's house was said to have stood. The foundations of this building have been dated to the 1st century AD, which matches the date when Mary is said to have left the Holy Land after the death of Jesus.

A mass is held every Sunday morning and Meryemana is always crowded at the Feast of the Assumption on 15 August. ⓐ Off route E87, 7 km (4 miles) south of Ephesus ◷ Open dawn–dusk ❶ Free admission to church but parking fee/entrance to compound

Selçuk Tourist office ⓐ Agora Çarşışı (across from the museum) ⓣ 0232 892 6328

Day Trip to Kos (Greece) ★★

The Knights of St John came here and built another castle just as impressive as the one at Bodrum, overlooking the harbour at Kos town, the capital of the island of Kos. The impressive Roman remains right in the centre of town were only discovered after an earthquake in 1933. Also visit the Hippocrates Tree – locals will tell you this is where the 'father of medicine,' a native of the island, would lecture to his students over 2500 years ago. The tree has proved to be one of the oldest in Europe, but sadly most experts believe that it is only 2000 years old and not of Hippocrates' era. ❶ The crossing from Bodrum takes around 90 minutes

If you want to do a spot of shopping, be aware that Greek shops close at lunch time.

LIFESTYLE
Aegean life

Food & drink

Turkish cuisine is considered to be one of the three greatest in the world. Just like French and Chinese cuisines, it has influenced both what we eat and how we eat it. Although the days of the great Ottoman banquets are long gone, Turks still make meal times an event.

Freshness is the key to Turkish food – you only have to look at the mountains of seasonal fruit and vegetables on sale in local markets or the seafood on ice at harbourfront restaurants for evidence of this. Dishes are generally cooked in olive oil and a range of herbs and spices has traditionally been used to add flavour, although these are never overpoweringly strong.

WHEN TO EAT

Turks take a very relaxed approach to mealtimes. There will always be somewhere open no matter what time you get hungry, although you will find a more lively atmosphere between noon and 14.30 for lunch and between 19.00 and 22.00 for dinner, when other people head out to eat. Only the most formal restaurants close between lunch and dinner and eateries of all kinds tend to stay open until the last client leaves.

WHERE TO EAT

Look out for the following different styles of eateries – depending on your appetite:

Kahve A Turkish coffee house that does not serve food and is usually a place for the men to get together for a game of backgammon or a gossip.

Lokanta A casual, often family-owned restaurant serving a small range of home-cooked dishes. There probably will not be a printed menu, but it is normal to go into the kitchen to see what is being cooked. Point at what you want if the staff do not speak English.

Turkish Delight and a cup of Çay

Restoran A more formal restaurant than a *lokanta*. A *restoran* will have a printed menu with prices.

Kebapçi Specializes in grilled meats. They vary from pretty, family-owned establishments with outdoor terraces to small, urban kiosks.

Meyhane A bar- or pub-style place serving meze with drinks. Traditionally these have been for males only, but in tourist areas women will also be welcomed.

Pideçi These small snack bars serve Turkish pizza.

Bufes A basic snack bar.

Pastane Turkish patisseries serving cakes and pastries.

TIPPING

Most *restoran* will add 10–15 per cent to your bill, but you should still leave a little something for the waiter. *Lokantas* will normally not add service to the bill. It is customary to leave 10–15 per cent. Leave small change on the table at bars and coffee houses.

WHAT TO EAT

Meze dishes or starters

Turks prefer to eat *meze* style. That is where several small dishes are served at once and shared by everyone around the table. Try eating *meze* style for a truly authentic experience or order these dishes as a starter.

Cold options include *yaprak dolması* (stuffed vine leaves), fresh olives, *imam bayildi* (slices of aubergine with tomatoes and onions in olive oil) and *cacık* (a refreshing dip of natural yoghurt and cucumber with a hint of mint). Warm *meze* dishes include *borek* (filo pastry squares filled with cheese and herbs) and *midye dolması* (stuffed mussels).

Because Turks eat *meze* style (see above) you may find that if you order starters and main courses they will both arrive together. To avoid this, order only one course at a time.

Main courses

The most popular form of main course is grilled or barbecued meat, usually lamb, but you will also find some beef. It is grilled as chops or steak but also cubed and skewered for *şiş kebabs*, thinly sliced for *döner kebabs* or minced for *köfte* (meat balls) or *İskender kebab* (minced meat wrapped around a skewer). Meat is always fresh and is generally served cooked through, not pink in the middle or rare.

Fresh fish is plentiful and delicious. You will find it elaborately displayed on ice at restaurant entrances. It is, however, always the most expensive item on the menu. It is sold by weight, so you choose a fish and it will be weighed and priced for you, then cooked to your specifications. If you find the price beyond your budget you get the chance to change your mind before it is too late.

You will normally find that your main meal comes with bread and salad and either rice or chips.

In Turkey, food is usually served warm rather than hot, which usually means that chips arrive soggy, not crisp. If you want yours piping hot, tell the waiter when you order.

Turkish mezes *are a popular option*

Snacks

Turkey has excellent pizza (*pide*, or *lahmacun*). It is lighter than the Italian variety and often served rolled up so you can eat it on the go. Equally delicious are *döner kebabs*, slivers of lamb wrapped with salad in pitta bread, which you can find on almost every street corner. *Gözleme* are pancakes or crepes with sweet or savoury fillings, while *semit* (bread rings sprinkled with sesame seeds) are perfect for stopping those afternoon hunger pangs.

Sweets

Turkish sweets and puddings are world renowned and make no apology for the amount of calories they contain. The most famous, *baklava* – layers of filo pastry soaked in butter, sprinkled with nuts then baked in honey syrup – is a work of art. Milk puddings are also popular, and are often delicious rich rice puddings evoking those we enjoyed as children.

Lokum, or Turkish Delight (a jelly sweet traditionally flavoured with rose water but made with many fruit flavours today), makes a great accompaniment to Turkish coffee. If all this really sounds a little over the top, most *lokanta* and *restoran* offer fresh melon or other seasonal fruit as a lighter but equally delicious end to your meal. The sweet toothed will need to head to a specialist café for dessert. These are often very basic establishments with vinyl-topped tables and fluorescent lights, so they do not get points for romantic ambience, but they are full of authentic atmosphere.

International food

More and more 'international' food has become available in Turkey. This includes all-day English breakfasts if that is what you want, as well as other familiar items like pizzas and burgers. If you want to splash out, the large, upmarket hotels will have formal and expensive restaurants serving 'continental' menus with silver service.

Turkish Çay (tea) is often served with a few sugar cubes

Drinks

Bottled water, the usual array of fizzy soft drinks and international spirits are readily available, so you will certainly find something familiar during your trip.

You may want to try a particularly Turkish beverage. *Khave*, or Turkish coffee, is strong but never harsh and served in small cups. Take it *sade* (no sugar), *az şekerli* (a little sugar) or *çok şekerli* (sweet), but never try to empty the cup because there are grounds in the bottom.

Çay (tea) is served weak without milk in tulip-shaped glasses. Apple tea is a refreshing alternative. Another delicious, non-alcoholic drink is *ayran*, a refreshing savoury natural yoghurt drink.

Turkey produces some excellent wine; look for the trade names *Doluca* and *Kavaklıdere* for quality and reliability. It also brews a good, clean-tasting Pilsen-type beer under the brand name *Efes*, but for something more potent try *raki*, an anise-based spirit that is diluted with water. It is drunk both as a before- and after-dinner drink, but at a strength of 40° should always be taken in moderation.

Here is how to say 'cheers' in Turkish: – *şerefe* (pronounced sheri-fey).

Menu decoder

A FEW BASIC WORDS

alabalık Freshwater trout
aşure Sweet 'soup' of fruits, nuts, pulses and bulgar wheat
balık Fish
barbunya Red mullet
beyti Minced kebab in pitta bread
bonfile Steak
borek Savoury pastry usually with cheese filling but can be meat
bülbül yuvası (swallow's nest) Shredded wheat in sugar syrup
çay Tea
çöp kebab Finely chopped meat or offal
dolma Vine leaves stuffed with rice and herbs
döner kebab Thin slices of grilled lamb sliced from a cone of meat
ekmek Bread
fasulye Haricot beans in tomato sauce
fırında sütlaç Oven-baked rice pudding usually served cold
gözleme A wafer-thin crepe with sweet or savoury filling
güllaç Flaky pastry and milk flavoured with nuts and rose water
güveç Meat and/or vegetable stew, cooked in a clay pot.
hamsi Anchovies
Haydarı Yoghurt dip flavoured with garlic
imam bayıldı Translated as 'the imam fainted' – a classic Ottoman dish of baked aubergine with tomatoes and onions served cold
istakoz Lobster
İskander kebab Minced meat cooked around a skewer and served in yoghurt or tomato sauce
kabak tatlısı Baked squash topped with clotted cream (*kaymak*)
kalamar Squid
karides Shrimp
karışık ızgara Mixed grill of lamb meat
karnıyarık Aubergines stuffed with minced lamb, currants and pine nuts then baked

karpuz Watermelon
kayısı Apricot
khave Turkish coffee
kiraz Cherry
kuzu Lamb
lahmacun A wafer-thin pizza topped with tomato sauce and minced lamb
levrek Sea bass
maden su Mineral water
manti Noodle dough ravioli parcels filled with meat
menemen Stir-fried omelette with hot peppers and vegetables
mercimak çorbası Lentil soup
midye Mussel
pastırma Dry-cured beef served thinly sliced
pide Small, flat pizzas with a thin topping of minced lamb or cheese
piliç Roast chicken
pirzola Lamb chops
pilav Rice
piyaz Haricot beans in vinaigrette
portakal Orange
salata Salad
şarap Wine
sardalya Sardine
sıgır Beef
siş kebab Cubes of meat put on a skewer then grilled
su Water
süt Milk
tarama Pink fish-roe paste
tavuk Boiled chicken
tel kadayıf Shredded wheat base smothered in honey syrup and chopped nuts
turşu Pickled vegetables
tuz Salt
yayla çorbası Rice soup
yoğurt çorbası Yoghurt soup

Shopping

Shopping in Aegean Turkey offers something for everyone, with a whole range of excellent souvenirs in all price brackets. You will be bombarded with designer 'rip-offs' offering those 'must-have names' at a fraction of the price back home. Stock up on items by your favourite fashion house but check merchandise carefully as quality varies from good to terrible.

Leather is one of the top 10 buys for tourists. You will find a fantastic range of bags, belts and jackets. Again, designer names predominate but you can find traditional styles or have something made just for you.

Turkey is famous for its handicrafts and these include inlaid wooden items like small tables or chess sets, copper pots, rustic ceramics and pottery, onyx or pipes carved from meerschaum, a soft, white clay-like material found only in Turkey.

Gold and silver jewellery is also good value since items such as chains and bracelets are priced by weight. You can have things made at small jewellery workshops within a few days. Gold is usually 14-carat quality. Always check for the hallmark on gold and silver items.

The prize souvenir has to be the handmade Turkish carpet. These have been woven for centuries, and each region has traditional patterns and colours. The best are made of silk but most are of wool.

Kilims are different from carpets because they have a flat weave rather than a pile. They are just as colourful but generally cheaper and they make great rugs and throws.

BROWSING

Browsing and window shopping are not something that the Turks do. When a shopkeeper sees you looking at his wares he assumes you have an interest in buying. They would rather you buy from them than the shop next door so they will put a lot of effort into getting you to stop, look and try.

BARTERING

Bartering or bargaining is a fact of life in Turkey. It is not something that comes naturally to a shopper who is used to fixed prices, but that does not mean that it is something to be nervous about. If you are in the market to buy an expensive souvenir, you will be paying well over the odds if you simply pay what the shopkeeper asks. There are several tips to make the bartering process more successful and enjoyable.

To start with, act cool about the specific item you want. Look at several items and then perhaps tell the shopkeeper you want to look in other shops to compare goods. You will be offered a drink – Turkish tea or a soft drink – and it shows that you are more serious about buying if you accept. Your first offer should be around 50 per cent, or half what the shop owner is asking, then increase your offer little by little. You will probably end up paying around 70 per cent of the original asking price, but early or late in the season it could be more. If you do not want to pay the price, simply tell the shop owner and walk away. He may call you back with a lower offer. Once you agree a price it is very bad manners to change your mind.

You will get a better price if you pay in cash not by credit card and better still if you pay in UK pounds or Euros than in Turkish Lira.

Turkish carpets are world famous and worth seeking out

Kids

Turkey is an ideal destination for children. The simple pleasures of guaranteed sunshine, excellent beaches and warm water to play in will keep them happy for hours. Add to this the child-friendly environment, where children are welcomed in restaurants and cafés, and it makes for a very relaxed holiday. Exuberance is not frowned upon here. Turks love children and allow them the freedom to enjoy their childhood.

That said, you will find fewer attractions specifically aimed at children than in many European destinations. There are no children's museums, few 'theme' parks and no games arcades. But the jet skiing and water rides make up for that, as well as the chance to spot a wild dolphin or turtle during a boat trip.

TIPS FOR A CHILD-FRIENDLY TRIP

Turkish excursions can be 'history' heavy and even some adults can tire of this. Pace the sightseeing so that you can alternate days of gazing at ancient buildings and tramping ancient streets with days by the pool or on the beach.

An afternoon siesta will help young children stay up late with the Turkish children – who are often still eating ice cream and playing in town squares until midnight. Early afternoon is also a good time to hide from the sun (see below).

BEACHES & ACTIVITIES

The best beaches in the region for children are the shallows of the southern Çeşme peninsula – Altınkum and Alaçatı (see pages 19 and 20) – as well as the good facilities of Ladies Beach and Pamaçuk at Kuşadası (see page 31), and the fine sand of Bitez (see page 53) or Gümbet close to Bodrum (see page 49).

All these offer a good range of water sports, which will suit active older children. They can take windsurfing lessons if they want to or just enjoy an exhilarating banana ride. For a gentler time it is possible to rent kayaks to explore the coastal shallows. Be aware that the winds around the Çeşme peninsula can be strong, so keep inexperienced windsurfers and kayakers under supervision. Kuşadası also has three large and modern water parks with rides for children of all ages, including safe areas for very young children.

On a totally different subject, the castles at Çeşme (see page 14) and Bodrum (see page 38) offer a chance for imaginations to run wild. Think 'swashbuckling' or 'Pirates of the Caribbean' and you have the idea.

TAKE CARE IN THE SUN

The Turkish sun is very hot and can damage young skin easily. Always make sure that children wear a high-factor sun cream. Reapply regularly and especially after they have been in the water. Limit children's time in the sun, especially from midday through the early afternoon, when the sun is at its strongest. Make sure they wear a hat and always carry a lightweight but long-sleeved garment for them in case their shoulders and arms need covering up. Keep children well hydrated – they may not complain of feeling thirsty, but will need lots of liquid to keep them well.

The shallow waters of Altinkum are perfect for children

Sports & activities

WATER SPORTS

You will not be short of water sports unless you choose a particularly quiet resort. From jet skiing to banana boat rides there is something for all the family.

SCUBA DIVING

The warm, clear waters around the Turkish coast make for great diving, but because of the many ancient remains lying in the coastal shallows, numerous locations remain off limits and divers must be accompanied by a registered Turkish guide or dive master. If you are already qualified, bring your certification with you in order to book a guide.

If you want to learn to dive, most large resorts have schools that are accredited by a Professional Association of Diving Instructors (PADI), where you can be assured of good-quality training.

Many schools also offer taster sessions for people who have never dived before. After some instruction you will be allowed to do a dive under strict supervision – this is a great introduction to the sport.

YACHTING

Getting out onto the water is a wonderful way to tour Turkey and a boat-based rather than a hotel-based package holiday is a popular and easy option. The most famous itinerary is the **Blue Voyage** (see page 41), but British-based holiday companies offer several different routes for one- or two-week stays. See **Sunsail** (ⓦ www.sunsail.co.uk) or **Moorings** (ⓦ www.moorings.co.uk) for more details.

If you do not want to spend your whole holiday at sea, try renting a boat, or a *gület* (a traditional wooden boat) for a day to sail off and find your own private cove or deserted beach. You can rent a boat with a crew at most marinas for a daily fee with lunch included. Although it is far more expensive than taking one of the many commercial boat tours (see opposite), it is still much better value than in other parts of the Mediterranean, and you have the whole boat to yourself.

Sailing on a Turkish gület is the ideal way to see the coastline

BOAT TRIPS

A huge flotilla of boats offers day trips and these are good value for money, with lunch and drinks included. It could be to a remote beach or a historic site, but all offer delightful panoramic views of the Turkish coastline and a chance to spot a dolphin or a turtle.

It pays to do a little research and price comparison. Check out what is included in the price before making a decision. Tickets usually need to be booked the day before.

CLIMBING

The Kaynaklar climbing area just outside Kaynaklar village is 45 km (28 miles) south-east of İzmir. There are set routes for experienced climbers, but no instruction, so it is not recommended for beginners.

WINDSURFING

The Aegean Coast benefits from perfect wind conditions with a prevailing north/south offshore breeze. Expert windsurfers flock to two centres of excellence, Alaçatı close to Çeşme (see page 20), and Bitez near Bodrum (see page 53), both of which hold international competitions. This is also a great place for beginners and improvers, with high-calibre instruction at both centres. All along the coast there are small schools offering lessons and board rentals. Kite surfing is also a sport that is growing in popularity.

Festivals & events

Turkey's festivals and events reflect its fascinating and unique society. A secular republic, it is very proud of its fight for independence, marking the major events with great solemnity. However, over 90 per cent of Turkey's population are Muslim, so they also celebrate the main Islamic festivals, especially in the countryside. On top of this, Turkey holds a whole host of sporting competitions and folkloric festivals.

CIVIL CELEBRATIONS

23 April National Sovereignty and Children's Day celebrates the establishment of the first Grand National Assembly in 1920, which saw the end of the Ottoman Empire.

19 May Atatürk Day and Youth and Sports Day marks the beginning of the Turkish War of Independence in 1919, when Atatürk rallied the country to fight the forces who had divided Turkish territory after World War I.

30 August Victory Day celebrates the success of Turkish forces over the Greek army in 1922.

29 October Republic Day marks the date when the present Turkish Republic was declared in 1923.

10 November Atatürk's Death: although not a holiday, Turks mark the day of Atatürk's death in a very poignant way. At 09.05 hours on 10 November, the exact time of his death, the whole country comes to a standstill for a minute of silent remembrance.

MAJOR MUSLIM CELEBRATIONS

The Muslim calendar runs on a lunar cycle different from that of our solar Gregorian calendar. These celebrations change date each year.

Ramadan (Ramazan)

For the entire ninth month (30 days) of the Muslim year, Muslims fast between dawn and dusk. This marks the time when Mohammed wandered in the desert and Allah revealed the verses of the Koran to him. Muslims devote Ramazan to prayer, reflection and charity.

Şeker Bayramı (She-ker Bay-ramer or the Sugar Festival)
This three-day festival celebrates the end of Ramazan. Families party together enjoying traditional foods, particularly sugary foods such as *baklava*, pastries and *lokum*.

Kurban Bayramı
The festival that commemorates the prophet Abraham offering his son Isaac to Allah or God (when Allah accepted the sacrifice of a sheep instead). It takes place during the tenth month of the Muslim year.

Other Muslim festivals
Other major and minor festivals are not necessarily holidays but are the times for special prayers and family get-togethers, including:
Aflure Günü (ah-shoo-reh gew-new) The tenth day of the Islamic lunar month of Muharrem commemorates Adam repenting his sin, the birth of the Prophet Abraham, Jonah's deliverance from the whale and the martyrdom of Islamic hero Hüseyin. Also, Turks celebrate Noah's ark coming to rest on dry land.
Mevlid-i Nebi (mehv-leed ee neh-bee) The Prophet Mohammed's birthday is celebrated with mosque illuminations and special foods.

Three other days of celebration where mosques are decorated and lit up are: **Regaip Kandili**, the 'Beginning of the Three Moons'; **Berat Kandili**, the 'Day of Forgiveness'; and **Miraç Kandili**, celebrating the Prophet Mohammed's ascent into heaven.

Circumcision ceremonies
Circumcision is an important milestone in the life of a young Turkish boy and takes place at any time between birth and the age of seven. The child is dressed in new clothes – often a bright satin suite and a light blue headdress, and then paraded around the town visiting family and friends. This was traditionally on horseback but today could be in a parade of cars that travels the streets with horns blaring. After the ceremony there is a big family party.

OTHER MAJOR EVENTS IN THE AEGEAN REGION

January

- Camel-wrestling Festival, Selçuk

April–May

- Festival of Cinema, Izmir

June

- Festival of Water Sports, Foça
- Surf and Sound Sport and Music festival, Alaçatı
- Turkish Windsurf Championship, Alaçatı

June–July

- **International Music Festival at Izmir –** performances also at Ephesus

July

- Çeşme hosts an annual International Song Contest

August

- Music and Folklore Festival, Ephesus
- Triathlon, Çeşme
- Feast of the Assumption, Meryemana
- (Church of the Virgin Mary), Selçuk

September

- **Liberation Day (9 Sept), Izmir** – when the Greek Army was ousted from the city in 1922
- **International Festival of Culture and Art, Bodrum** – events are held along Neyzen Tevfik Caddesi and in the castle compound

October

- **The Bodrum Cup** – professional yachting competitions

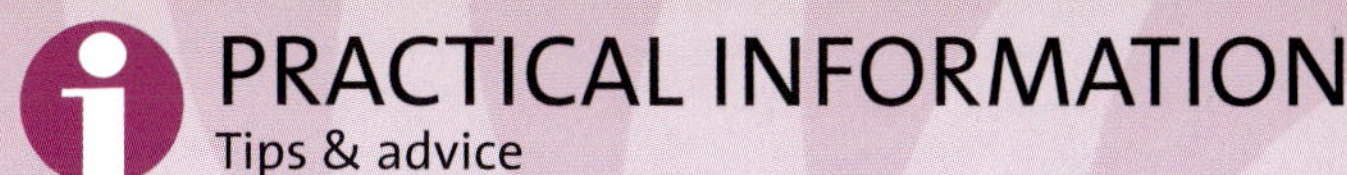

PRACTICAL INFORMATION

Tips & advice

Preparing to go

GETTING THERE

Turkey is a popular destination and features in the brochures of all the major package tour operators with a range of hotels and holidays in all price brackets. Prices are highest when demand is high, such as during school holiday periods, when it is wise to book as early as possible, especially of you have children.

If you are more flexible, it will be less busy and cheaper to travel early (May/June) or late in the season (September/October), when last-minute bargains are possible. Teletext, the Internet or travel agents offer ways to compare prices and facilities whatever time of year you want to travel. If you want to organize your own package you can book a scheduled flight (flexible dates) or charter flight (fixed dates of one or two weeks' duration) and find your own accommodation. Many hotels have their own websites that allow you to make and confirm booking, or use specialist companies such as **Expedia** (Ⓦ www.expedia.co.uk), **Travelocity** (www.travelocity.co.uk) or **Priceline** (www.priceline.co.uk).

You should also check the travel supplements of the weekend newspapers such as the *Sunday Telegraph* and *Sunday Times*. They often carry adverts for inexpensive flights and privately owned villas and apartments to rent.

By air

You have the choice of two airports when you travel to the Turkish Aegean. Both **Izmir Adnan Menderes International** in the north and **Bodrum/Milas** in the south take charter flights from many UK airports during the holiday season (April–October).

There are no direct international scheduled flights to either airport. You will need to take a flight to Istanbul and then fly out to Izmir or Bodrum with **Turkish Airlines** (Ⓦ www.turkishairlines.com), the national airline. It operates several flights a day to both locations all year round.

Both airports have duty-free shops, exchange bureaux, car-rental offices and taxis, but services are limited if you arrive or depart at night.

TOURIST INFORMATION

For more information about Turkey before you leave, contact the **Turkish Culture and Tourism Office** (ⓐ 170–173 Piccadilly, London W1J 9EJ ⓣ 0207 629 7771 ⓕ 0207 491 0773 ⓦ www.gototurkey.co.uk).

BEFORE YOU LEAVE

Holidays are supposed to be relaxing, so take a little time and plan ahead. You do not need inoculations to travel to Turkey but it would be wise to make sure that your family is up to date with shots like tetanus. It is also worth having a dental check-up before you go.

It is sensible to carry a small first-aid kit with items such as painkillers, treatment for upset stomachs, travel/sea-sickness tablets, plasters, antiseptic ointment and insect repellent. Sun cream is more expensive in Turkey, so buy this before you go. If you take any prescription medication make sure you have enough for the duration of your holiday.

DOCUMENTS

The most important documents you will need are tickets and passports. Make sure that passports for all members of the family are up to date. Children already named on a parent's passport can travel without their own passports, but any recent additions to the family or children not on a passport already will need to have their own. These can take up to 28 days to be issued by the passport office, although you can pay more for a quicker service. If your passport has less than three months to run on the date you arrive in Turkey, you need to renew it before you go. For further information on how to renew you passport and for current processing times, get in touch with the **Passport Agency** (ⓣ 0870 521 0410 or ⓦ www.ukpa.gov.uk). When your tickets arrive from the travel agent check that all the names, dates and times are correct.

Keep passports and travel tickets or confirmations in a safe place. If possible keep photocopies of your passport numbers and ticket information (and travellers' cheques if you take them) separately.

If you are going to hire a car while in Turkey all named drivers need to have their driver's licences with them.

MONEY

Always change a small amount of currency before you leave, especially if your flight arrives late in the evening or early in the morning. You can do this at a post office, travel agent (allow two or three days for the money to arrive) or at the airport just before you fly. Make sure that your credit and debit cards are up to date before you travel.

Changing money Banks can be found in all major towns. There are plenty of exchange bureaux in resorts. Before you change money check the exchange and commission rates. You will find cashpoints in the larger resorts, but not all smaller resorts have them.

Travellers' cheques Provide the safest way to carry money since they can be replaced if lost or stolen (remember to note down the cheque numbers in the event of needing to have them replaced). Order them from a bank or travel agent at least a week before you leave on holiday. Travellers' cheques can be cashed at banks, exchange bureaux and many hotels.

ATM machines These are widespread in the resort areas. You can obtain cash with either your Maestro Card or credit card provided you have a Personal Identification Number (PIN). Your bank or credit card company may charge more for this service.

Credit cards These are becoming more widely accepted in shops and restaurants but not in cheaper *lokantas* and *pide* stalls or in the markets, so do not rely on this as your only method of payment.

You can often pay in pounds rather than in Turkish Lira, so it pays to take some British cash; remember to keep this secure.

INSURANCE

Check that your insurance policy covers you adequately for loss of possessions and valuables, for activities you might want to try – such as horse-riding or water sports – and for emergency medical and dental treatment, including flights home, if required. Note also that UK visitors are not entitled to reduced-cost or free medical treatment, as Turkey is not, at the time of writing, a part of the EEA.

CLIMATE

The coastal areas of western Turkey have a Mediterranean climate. This means long, hot dry summers, mild winters with some rain and short, warm springs and autumns.

Average daytime temperatures are: April – 20°C (68°F); May – 24°C (75°F); June – 29°C (84°F); July – 31°C (88°F); August – 32°C (90°F); September – 29°C (84°F); October – 24°C (75°F).

In summer you will only need light clothing – breathable and natural fabrics are best – but take lightweight trousers and a long-sleeved shirt to cover your arms and legs in case you get sunburnt.

Early or late in the season take a warmer layer like a light fleece just in case it gets a bit chilly in the evenings.

SECURITY

Take sensible precautions while you are away:

- Make sure your burglar alarm is working.
- Consult a Neighbourhood Watch scheme if there is one in your area.
- Cancel regular deliveries such as milk and newspapers.
- Let the postman know you will not be there to receive bulky post.
- Ask a neighbour to keep an eye on your home and perhaps pull the curtains closed in the evenings. Security features such as timers can be used to switch lights on and off to make it look as though someone is at home.

AIRPORT PARKING & ACCOMMODATION

Book airport parking or overnight accommodation close to the airport as soon as you have booked your holiday. Demand for both is high, especially in the summer. Some hotels offer free parking for a one- or two-week holiday if you book rooms with them.

BAGGAGE ALLOWANCES

Baggage allowances are becoming more strict and the price of excess baggage (that over the amount allowed as part of your ticket) is expensive. Currently scheduled flights allow 20 kg (44 lb) of checked-in baggage (bags that go into the hold) per passenger, but charter flights have lower limits, as little as 15 kg (33 lb) for clients who have booked at the last minute or bought a flight-only package. Your tour company will tell you your limit and it will be printed on your ticket. Each passenger is also allowed to carry a small bag (5 kg/11 lb) onto the plane, plus duty-free shopping and items such as laptop computers or cameras.

If you think you may want to take more than this allowance, ask about buying extra baggage capacity before you travel (preferably at the same time as you book your ticket). Many airlines can sell extra capacity to you that will be much less expensive than would be the case if you just turned up at the check-in desk with overweight bags.

If you are going to be travelling with a large item – a push-chair, golf clubs or surf board, for example – let the holiday company know when you make the booking. There may be an extra charge for these.

The prices of some items, such as spirits and cigarettes, can be less expensive in Turkey than in the duty-free shops at the airport.

CHECK-IN, PASSPORT CONTROL & CUSTOMS

For first-time travellers, airport procedures and security can be a little intimidating but the process is simple and straightforward.

Check-in desks usually open two or three hours before a flight is scheduled to leave. Leave the house so that you arrive early at the airport. This will give you a good choice of seat and help avoid any unforeseen delay en route that will make you miss your flight. Most airports have good restaurant and café facilities and it is better to wait in them for your flight time rather than to stress over being late. You can always use this time to read up on your holiday destination.

Look for your flight number on the TV monitors in the check-in area and find the relevant check-in desk. Your tickets will be checked and your luggage taken. Take your boarding card and go to the departure lounge through the security check area. Here your hand luggage will be x-rayed and your passport checked.

In the departure lounge, you can still shop for duty-free goods, but watch the monitors that tell you when to board – usually about 30 minutes before take-off. Go to the departure gate shown and follow the instructions given you by the airline staff.

Because Turkey is outside the EU you will be allowed to purchase goods 'duty free'. You will not be allowed to take more than the following amounts of duty-free goods into Turkey:

- 200 cigarettes or 50 cigars or 200g of tobacco
- 5 litres (9 pt) of alcohol

During your stay

AIRPORTS

There is good road access to the region's airports, but if you are returning a rental car at the end of your holiday allow plenty of time to reach the airport and check in for your flight. If your flight departs at night the airport will have limited facilities during your wait so it might be wise to take drinks and snacks. Also, duty-free shops may not be open at night.

CURRENCY

In January 2005, Turkey devalued its currency and issued new notes and coins. The Yeni (New) Turkish Lira or YTL replaced the old Turkish Lira, and each new Lira is worth 1,000,000 old Lira. Yeni Lira come in note denominations of 1, 5, 10, 20, 50 and 100 Lira. Each Yeni Lira is made up of 100 Kuruş, which come in coins of 1, 5, 10, 25 and 50 Kuruş. There is also a 1 Lira coin.

ELECTRICITY

Power is 220 volts, 50 cycles. Plugs are European style with two round pins so you will need an adapter for your electrical appliances.

EMBASSIES & CONSULATES

The **British Embassy** is located in the Turkish capital Ankara ⓐ Sehit Ersan Caddesi 46/A, Çankaya, Ankara ⓣ 0312 455 3344

There are also local consular contacts in the Aegean at **British Consul Izmir** ⓐ 1442 Sokak No 49, Alsancak, Izmir PK 300 ⓣ 0232 463 5151 **British Honorary Consul Bodrum** ⓐ Kibris Sehitleri Caddesi, Konacik Mevkii, 401/B, Bodrum ⓣ 0252 319 0093/94

FACILITIES FOR VISITORS WITH DISABILITIES

Turkey is working hard to improve facilities for the disabled but provision is still patchy. Many newly built hotels and public buildings have facilities but access to archaeological sites and historic buildings is difficult and the lack of curb ramps and controlled street crossings in towns makes movement problematical. If necessary, contact the hotels direct to ensure that they can provide what you need. For further help, contact **Holiday Care International** – they have information about facilities and accessibility in destinations for travellers with disabilities. ⓐ 7th Floor, Sunley House, 4 Bedford Park, Croydon, Surrey CR0 2AP ⓣ 0845 124 9971 ⓦ www.holidaycare.org.uk

GETTING AROUND

Car hire The easiest way to rent a car is to book it in the UK at the same time as you book your holiday. This way you can be clear about costs and correct insurance cover. It is also easy to rent a car in Turkey if you decide you want a couple of days or more on the road. At your resort, your representative will be able to help you, or visit a local car-rental office. Check the quality of the cars before you rent.

You will need to leave a deposit and show your driving licence. For all car rentals, make sure you get a contact telephone number in case you have mechanical problems. Drivers must be over 21 years of age (some companies 25 years) and have held a full licence for at least a year.

TELEPHONING TURKEY

To call Turkey from the UK, dial 00 90 followed by the area code (minus the initial 0), then the 7-digit number.

Driving In Turkey you drive on the right and overtake on the left (the opposite of the UK). Speed limits are 50 km/h (31 mph) in urban areas, 90 km/h (56 mph) on main roads and 120 km/h (75 mph) on motorways and dual carriageways – unless the signs indicate another limit. Seat belts are compulsory in front seats and back seats where fitted.

The main coast road and other major roads are generally in good condition, but small roads vary in quality and some are dirt surface rather than asphalt.

You will meet all kinds of traffic on the roads, from large, modern trucks to donkey and carts (and the occasional loose farm animal). You will need to be on the alert for slower moving vehicles. Slower traffic will usually move onto the hard shoulder to allow you to pass.

If Turkish drivers want to cross the traffic, they will often pull over to the right and let traffic behind them pass before making the turn so they do not hold everyone up.

When traffic is quieter (at night and on Sundays), Turkish traffic lights are switched to flashing amber. This means that you will need to pay attention because there is a junction or crossroads ahead that is not controlled.

Parking is a problem in all the major resorts. Do not park where you see a yellow kerb.

You will find both leaded and unleaded petrol. Not all fuel stations are self-service. A member of staff may come and clean your windscreen. This is at no extra cost, but staff will appreciate a small tip. Some petrol stations do not accept credit cards.

Public transport Long distance bus services – all Turkish towns and cities are served by an efficient, modern and cheap bus network that makes an excellent framework for touring. Services feature air conditioning, videos (in Turkish, of course), refreshments and programmed stops for meals.

Local buses The *dolmuş* is the lifeblood of local transport. These small mini-vans run set routes, leaving the terminus when full and picking up passengers anywhere along the route. There will usually be a service from town to the main beaches and resort hotels. They are cheap and efficient.

HEALTH MATTERS

Should you require medical help, most hotels will have a doctor on call but you will be charged for the consultation (you can usually claim this back from your holiday insurance policy).

Hospital If you need to stay in hospital there are clean, though limited, facilities in most large towns, smaller clinics in smaller towns. Staff are well trained and most doctors can speak some English. You have to pay for treatment but depending on circumstances this could be organized directly through your insurance company. If you have travelled on a package holiday with a major tour company, your resort representative will be able to offer advice and help.

Pharmacies (Ezcane) Pharmacists in Turkey are highly qualified and most will speak some English. They will be able to advise you on treatments for complaints such as minor sunburn, upset tummy, insect bites and diarrhoea. Normal opening hours are from 09.00 to 19.00 hours and there will be a duty pharmacist available in every town.

Water Although tap water is clean, only drink bottled or boiled water.

THE LANGUAGE

Turkish is a relatively new language. It was developed in the 1920s by Kemal Atatürk, the first President of the Turkish Republic, to replace Arabic. It uses the Latin alphabet. Every letter in each Turkish word is pronounced, even when there is a double letter such as in the word '*saat*' (hour), so you would say 'sa-at'. All letters are pronounced as in English except the following:

c which is pronounced as a 'j' as in 'Jerry'
ç which is pronounced 'ch' as is 'chaffinch'
ğ which is a silent or soft g, it lengthens the sound of the letter before it
ı (a dotless ı) and is pronounce 'a' as in the first syllable of 'another'
ö as in the 'u' in fur
ş pronounced 'sh' as in 'ship'
ü pronounced as the French 'tu'

ENGLISH	**TURKISH**
Useful words & phrases	
Hello	*merhaba*
Good morning	*günaydin*
Good evening	*iyi akşamlar*
Good night	*iyi geceler*
Goodbye (said by those departing)	*allahaısmarladık*
Goodbye (said by those remaining)	*güle güle*
Yes	*evet*
No	*yok or hayir*
Please	*lutfen*
Thank you	*mersi or teşekkur ederim*
Do you speak English?	*Ingilizce biliyormusunuz*
I don't understand	*anlamıyorum*
I understand	*anlıyorum*
I don't know	*bilmiyorum*
The bill	*hesap*
General Vocabulary	
Bus	*autobüs*
Small local bus	*dolmüş*
Ferry	*feribot*
Port	*limani*
Plane	*uçak*
Airport	*hava limani*
Ladies (toilet)	*bayanlar*
Mens (toilet)	*baylar*
Left	*sağa*
Right	*sola*
Straight ahead	*doşdogru*
How much is this?	*ne kadar or ne kaça*
Money (cash)	*para*
Too expensive	*çok pahalı*

ENGLISH	**TURKISH**
Travellers' cheques	*seyahat çeki*
Do you sell stamps?	*Posta pulu var mı?*
Open	*açik*
Postage stamp	*pul*
Closed	*kapalı*
Credit card	kredi kartı
Today	*bugün*
Yesterday	*dün*
Tomorrow	*yarın*
Where is?	*nerede*
Mosque	*cami*
Market or bazaar	*çarşı*
Mountain	*daş*
Street	*sokak* (often abbreviated to *sok*)
Avenue	caddesi (often abbreviated to *cad*)
Place	meydani (often abbreviated to *meyd*)
Boulevard	*Bulvari* (abbreviated to *Bul*)
Call the police!	*polise haber verin!*
What time is it?	*saat kaç?*
Duty pharmacy	*nöbeçi ezcane*
Doctor	*doktor*
Emergency exit	*imdat Çikişi*
Hospital	*hastane*
Room	*oda*
Toilet	*tuvalet*
Shower	*duş*
Towel	*havlu*

Numbers

One	*bir*
Two	*iki*
Three	*üç*

ENGLISH	TURKISH
Four	*dört*
Five	*beş*
Six	*altı*
Seven	*yedi*
Eight	*sekiz*
Nine	*dokuz*
Ten	*on*
One hundred	*yüz*
One thousand	bin
Days of the week	
Monday	*pazartezi*
Tuesday	*salı*
Wednesday	*çarşamba*
Thursday	*perşembe*
Friday	*cuma*
Saturday	*cumartesi*
Sunday	*pazar*

LOST PROPERTY

If it is possible, retrace your steps. Turks are honest people by nature and someone may have your lost item in safe-keeping for you.

- If you have a representative, report the matter to them and ask for their advice.
- Visit the nearest police station to report your loss.
- Report any lost credit cards to the credit card company immediately.
- Report any lost passport to your nearest embassy or consulate immediately.

MAKING A COMPLAINT

If you want to make a complaint about anything that happens during your holiday, explain as simply as you can what the problem is. Stay calm

and do not lose your temper. Your holiday representative is there to help make your holiday as enjoyable as possible. See them for any complaint about flight or hotel. In restaurants or shops, ask to speak to the manager or owner.

MEDIA

The only English-language newspaper printed in Turkey is the *Turkish Daily News*. The popular English tabloids are widely available in all the leading resorts at a price premium, though they may be a day old. Most upmarket hotels will offer BBC *News 24* as part of their programming. Resort bars will often transmit Premier League matches live, and show English news reports. You will find Internet cafés in most resorts.

OPENING HOURS

Banks 08.30–noon and 13.30–17.00 (Mon–Fri)
Shops 09.00–19.00 (Mon–Sat); tourist shops daily 09.00–22.00 in the resorts in summer
Government offices 08.30–12.30 and 13.30–17.30 (Mon–Fri)
State museums 08.30–17.30 (Tues–Sun); closed for lunch in winter
Archaeological sites 08.00–18.00 or 19.00 in summer
Warning Opening hours for museums and archaeological sites change all the time. It is probably best not to arrive too early or too late at a site in case the ticket office is closed

POST OFFICES

Post offices have yellow signs with the black letters PTT. Most are open government office hours and offer postal and telecommunications services. Shops selling postcards may also sell stamps.

PUBLIC TOILETS

There are few public toilet facilities in Turkey. The best policy is to stop at a café or bar. If in a resort, visit the nearest hotel. Always carry a supply of toilet roll or tissue, as few toilets outside the hotels will have any. In museums and archaeological sites you may have to pay a small amount for use of the facilities. Keep small change handy for this.

RELIGION

Turkey is a predominantly Muslim country although it is one of the most liberal Islamic populations in the world. Alcohol and gambling are allowed. The countryside is generally more conservative then the coastal resorts. If you are travelling away from the coast, or wanting to visit mosques or churches, modest dress is appropriate.

SAFETY & SECURITY

Turkey is a safe country and you are very unlikely to find yourself the victim of a serious incident. However, petty crime such as theft can be guarded against with a few simple rules.

- Do not carry large amounts of cash or valuables with you. Take only what you need for the day.
- Do not leave anything on show in your hire car.
- Do not leave valuables unguarded on the beach or in cafés.
- Keep to well-lit streets at night.
- If unsure of the route back to your hotel or apartment take a taxi.
- Report any stolen credit cards to the credit card company immediately.
- Report any stolen passport to your nearest embassy or consulate immediately.

TELEPHONES

Most resorts have modern public phone boxes that offer international direct dialling to the UK. Phone boxes operate with major credit cards or phone cards that can be purchased at press kiosks, tourist offices and

EMERGENCY TELEPHONE NUMBERS

- **Police** 155
- **Ambulance** 112

TELEPHONING ABROAD

To call an overseas number from Turkey, dial 00 followed by the country code (UK=44) and the area code (minus the initial 0), then the rest of the number.

USEFUL TELEPHONE NUMBERS

- **Long distance operator** 131
- **International reverse charge calls** 115
- **International directory enquiries** 161

post offices. Your personal portable phone should also work, although the cost of calls is a lot higher than at home. Check this out with your service provider before you leave. Most upmarket and resort hotels offer international direct dialling that allows you to phone home from your room. ❶ Hotels often charge a high premium; ask about rates in advance.

TIME DIFFERENCES

Turkey is two hours ahead of Greenwich Mean Time (GMT).

TIPPING

In restaurants, it is advisable to leave 10–15 per cent of the bill, plus small change for the waiter. In cafés and bars, leave a tip of small change. Bell-boys should receive one 50 Kuru (see Currency, page 115) per bag, room cleaners should be left 50 Kuru per day, and shoe guardians in mosques welcome a small tip.

WEIGHTS & MEASUREMENTS

Turkey uses the metric system, which uses grams and kilograms, milli-litres and litres, metres and kilometres.

INDEX

ACKNOWLEDGEMENTS

We would like to thank all the photographers, picture libraries and organizations for the loan of the photographs reproduced in this book, to whom copyright in the photograph belongs:
Jupiter Images Corporation (pages 109, 125);
Thomas Cook Tour Operations Ltd (pages 1, 5, 11, 12, 18, 22, 25, 30, 34, 37, 43, 44, 48, 52, 55, 57, 60, 63, 73, 87, 89, 92, 95, 101, 102, 105).

We would also like to thank the following for their contribution to this series:
John Woodcock (map and symbols artwork);
Becky Alexander, Patricia Baker, Sophie Bevan, Judith Chamberlain-Webber, Stephanie Evans, Nicky Gyopari, Krystyna Mayer, Robin Pridy (editorial support);
Christine Engert, Suzie Johanson, Richard Lloyd, Richard Peters, Alistair Plumb, Jane Prior, Barbara Theisen, Ginny Zeal, Barbara Zuñiga (design support)

Send your thoughts to
books@thomascook.com

- **Found a beach bar, peaceful stretch of sand or must-see sight that we don't feature?**
- **Like to tip us off about any information that needs a little updating?**
- **Want to tell us what you love about this handy, little guidebook and more importantly how we can make it even handier?**

Then here's your chance to tell all! Send us ideas, discoveries and recommendations today and then look out for your valuable input in the next edition of this title. And, as an extra 'thank you' from Thomas Cook Publishing, you'll be automatically entered into our exciting monthly prize draw.

Email to the above address or write to:
HotSpots Project Editor, Thomas Cook Publishing, PO Box 227, Unit 15/16, Coningsby Road, Peterborough PE3 8SB, UK.